GLUTEN-FREE
COOKBOOK

Penguin
Random
House

Project editor Elizabeth Yeates
Designer Alison Shackleton
Senior jacket creative Mark Penfound
Pre-production producer Andy Hilliard
Producer Konrad Kirkham
Special sales creative project manager Alison Donovan

Photography William Shaw

Important Every effort has been made to ensure that the information contained in this book is complete and accurate. However, neither the publisher nor the authors are engaged in rendering professional advice or services to the individual reader. Professional medical advice should be obtained on personal health matters. Neither the publisher nor the authors accept any legal responsibility for any personal injury or other damage or loss arising from the use or misuse of the information and advice in this book.

First published in Great Britain 2015 by
Dorling Kindersley Limited
80 Strand, London WC2R 0RL

Material previously published in *The Gluten-Free Cookbook* (2012)

A CIP catalogue record for this book
is available from the British Library
ISBN 978-0-2412-0091-9

Printed in China

All images © Dorling Kindersley Limited
For further information see: **www.dkimages.com**

A WORLD OF IDEAS:
SEE ALL THERE IS TO KNOW

CONTENTS

ELIMINATING GLUTEN

WHAT IS GLUTEN?

Gluten is a protein found in wheat, rye, and barley and in foods made from these grains, such as cakes, pastry, bread, and pasta. Gluten has qualities useful for cooking and baking, including elasticity, an ability to hold water, and a tendency to hold shape and harden in high heat.

WHAT DOES GLUTEN DO?

It is the gluten in flour that gives bread and baked goods, such as cakes and muffins, their characteristic texture and structure. When flour is mixed with water the gluten becomes elastic, turning the mixture into a soft, stretchy dough that can be kneaded and shaped. Carbon dioxide produced by yeast or baking powder is trapped within the dough and held there by the gluten, enabling breads and cakes to rise and giving them their "airy" texture. Thanks to a miraculous little ingredient called xanthan gum, however, it's possible to mimic the action of gluten in doughs made with gluten-free flours. And by carefully mixing the different gluten-free flours available, and adding additional flavours and glazes, it is possible to recreate the taste, texture, and appearance of all your favourite bakes in gluten-free form. See page 24 for flour blends.

Gluten-containing grains

Cultivated grains containing gluten are limited to wheat, spelt (an ancient form of wheat), barley, and rye. Triticale, a hybrid of wheat and rye, also contains gluten and can be found in some health food shops, but is mainly used as an animal feed.

MAIN GLUTEN-CONTAINING PRODUCTS

- All biscuits, breads, cakes, chapattis, crackers, muffins, pastries, pizza bases, rolls, and scones made from wheat, rye, or barley flour
- Wheat noodles and pasta
- Wheat-based breakfast cereals
- Meat and poultry cooked in batter or breadcrumbs, e.g. breaded ham, faggots, haggis, rissoles, Scotch eggs
- Fish or shellfish coated in batter or breadcrumbs, e.g. fish cakes, fish fingers
- Fromage frais and yogurt containing muesli or cereals
- Vegetables and fruit in batter, breadcrumbs, or dusted with flour
- Potatoes in batter, breadcrumbs, or dusted with flour, e.g. potato croquettes
- Soy sauce
- Ice cream cones and wafers, puddings made using semolina or wheat flour
- Stuffing made from breadcrumbs

CAN I EAT OATS ON A GLUTEN-FREE DIET?

Oats contain a protein similar to gluten but it doesn't seem to cause the same adverse reaction. Coeliacs wishing to introduce oats into their diet should start by adding small amounts, but children and severe sufferers should consult their dietitian first. Oats are often contaminated with gluten during processing, so buy gluten-free brands.

WHEAT »
Triticum spp.

Wheat varieties often have different names: Emmer, Kamut, Einkorn, Faro, Farrina, and Dinkel are all types of wheat. Bulgur wheat (pictured), couscous, and semolina are also made from wheat.

« BARLEY
Hordeum vulgare

Pearl barley can be added to stews and barley flakes are sometimes added to muesli. Beer, barley waters or squash, and malted milk drinks all contain barley.

RYE »
Secale cereale

Rye bread and pumpernickel are popular in Germany and eastern Europe. Rye is also used to make crisp breads and crackers.

« SPELT
Triticum spelta

An ancient form of wheat that has seen a resurgence in popularity in recent years as a health food. Used in baked goods and beer.

Finding hidden gluten

Eliminating gluten from your diet is not as simple as cutting out obvious sources of gluten, such as bread and pasta. Wheat and other gluten-containing grains are often used as ingredients in other foods, and in some cases foods that are naturally gluten free can become contaminated with gluten during processing or storage. For this reason it's important to check the label on certain products and choose brands certified gluten free where contamination is a risk, such as with oats and polenta.

PRODUCTS THAT MAY CONTAIN HIDDEN GLUTEN

Check closely the packaging of food products listed here for the presence of hidden gluten.

GRAINS AND FLOURS
Sometimes naturally gluten-free grains are milled with wheat, barley, or rye and are thereby contaminated with gluten. These include: buckwheat, chestnut, chickpea, gram, millet, mustard, oats, polenta, potato, quinoa, rice, sorghum, soya, tapioca, teff, and urad

BREAKFAST CEREALS
Buckwheat, corn, millet, and rice-based breakfast cereals and those that contain barley malt extract or oats

PRESERVES AND SPREADS
Lemon curd, mincemeat, peanut and other nut butters

FRUITS AND VEGETABLES
Fruit pie fillings and processed vegetable dishes made with sauces, such as cauliflower cheese

SOUPS AND SAUCES
Canned or packet soups, sauces in jars and packets

Blended seasonings, gravy granules, stock cubes, curry powder, curry paste

Mustard products such as English mustard

Chutneys and pickles

Dressings, salad cream, and mayonnaise

DRINKS
Cloudy fizzy drinks, drinking chocolate, malted milk

DAIRY AND FATS
Coffee and tea whiteners

Fruit and flavoured yogurts or fromage frais desserts

Soya desserts, rice milk, soya milk

Some soft, spreadable cheeses

BAKING INGREDIENTS
Cake decorations, marzipan, ready-to-use icing

Baking powder, bicarbonate of soda

Suet, vegetarian suet

CHECKING THE LABEL

The names of some additives used by the food industry can hide the fact they are derived from gluten grains and may not be safe. Look out for the following:

✗ **Rusk** made from wheat flour is often used as a carrier for flavours and colours.

✗ **Cereal fillers** made from breadcrumbs, or wheat flour are often added to foods like sausages.

✗ **Cereal or vegetable proteins** are flavour enhancers that can be derived from wheat.

✗ **Starch**, whether "modified", "food" or "edible" can be made from wheat or rye. Often used as thickeners.

✗ **Malt extract or flavouring** is used in baking and brewing and derives from malted barley.

INGREDIENTS TO AVOID: ...**Cereal filler**...**Starch**...**Modified starch**...**Food starch**...**Edible starch**...**Cereal protein**...**Vegetable protein**...**Rusk**...**Bran**...**Malt extract**...**Malt flavouring**...

SAFE WHEAT-DERIVED INGREDIENTS: ...**Glucose**...**Dextrose**...**Glucose powder**...**Glucose syrup**...**Maltodextrin**...**Codex wheat starch**...**Monosodium glutamate (MSG)**...

✔ See page 8 for information on **Codex wheat starch** and **MSG**.

✔ **Dextrose and glucose**, including powder and syrup, are flavour and texture enhancers that can be made from the starch of wheat and barley. They are safe for coeliacs because they contain so little protein.

✔ **Maltodextrin** is an additive used in soft drinks and sweets that can be derived from wheat. Most of the protein is first removed, making it safe for coeliacs.

NUTS AND SAVOURY SNACKS
Dry roasted nuts, popcorn (not home-made), potato and vegetable crisps, pretzels

Baked beans and other beans in sauce

POTATO PRODUCTS
Frozen chips and potato wedges, instant mash, potato waffles, ready-to-roast potatoes

MEAT AND FISH
Any meat or poultry marinated or in a sauce, burgers, meat pastes, pâtés, sausages

Fish pastes, fish pâtés, taramasalata, and fish in sauce

MEATLESS ALTERNATIVES
Marinated tofu, soya mince, falafel, vegetable burgers and bean burgers

CAKES AND BISCUITS
Shop-bought meringues, macaroons, and flapjacks are likely to have come into contact with gluten-containing cakes

CONFECTIONERY AND DESSERTS
Chocolates, ice cream, mousses, and all kinds of sweets, especially liquorice sweets

TO EAT OR NOT TO EAT? – A QUICK Q&A

You should now have a good sense of which foods to avoid completely and which to check first, but there will inevitably be many more questions as you examine your diet. Here we try to answer the most common ones. For a comprehensive list of safe products it is a good idea to buy Coeliac UK's annual Food and Drink Directory.

IS IT SAFE TO EAT FOODS COOKED IN THE SAME OIL USED TO FRY FOODS COATED IN GLUTEN BATTERS OR CRUMB COATINGS?

No. The oil can be contaminated with gluten from batter used to coat fish and other foods. Look out for gluten-free evenings, however, which are becoming popular with local fast food outlets, when they use gluten-free batter and clean oil to prevent cross contamination.

ARE PRODUCTS LABELLED AS WHEAT-FREE SUITABLE FOR SOMEONE ON A GLUTEN-FREE DIET?

Not necessarily. Wheat is not the only gluten-containing grain and the product may still have rye- or barley-based ingredients, or oats contaminated with gluten.

WHAT IS CODEX WHEAT STARCH?

Codex wheat starch is added to processed foods to improve their taste and texture. Though made from wheat, it has been processed to contain less than 20 parts per million (ppm) of gluten. Research shows this tiny amount of gluten is not toxic to coeliacs.

IS MONOSODIUM GLUTAMATE (MSG) GLUTEN FREE?

MSG is a flavour enhancer used in many ready meals, stock cubes, and savoury snacks and can be made from wheat. However, during processing the gluten protein is completely broken down, so MSG is safe for people with coeliac disease.

DO SOME MEDICINES AND SUPPLEMENTS CONTAIN GLUTEN?

Most medicines and drugs prescribed in the UK are gluten free. Although they can sometimes contain wheat starch as a filler, it is highly processed and safe for anyone on a gluten-free diet. If you are buying non-prescription medicines and supplements, however, you should check with a pharmacist.

CAN I USE MALT VINEGAR?

Although malt vinegar is made from barley, the end product only contains a trace amount of gluten, well below the level that is safe for most people with coeliac disease, and is fine to use. Balsamic, cider, sherry, white wine, and red wine vinegars are all safe.

Naturally gluten-free foods

The idea of cutting gluten out of your diet can seem slightly daunting, but all the foods listed here are naturally gluten-free and can still be enjoyed.

MEAT, POULTRY, AND FISH »
- All fresh meats and poultry
- Cured pure meats, plain cooked meats, smoked meats
- All fresh, dried, kippered, and smoked fish, fish canned in brine, oil or water, and shellfish

« FRUIT, VEGETABLES, NUTS, AND SEEDS
- All fresh, frozen, canned, dried, and juiced pure fruits and vegetables
- Vegetables pickled in vinegar
- All plain potatoes, baked, steamed, boiled, or mashed
- Plain nuts and seeds, all pulses (peas, beans, lentils)

DAIRY, EGGS, AND FATS »
- All milk (liquid and dried), all cream (single, double, whipping, clotted, soured, and crème fraîche), buttermilk, plain fromage frais, plain yogurt
- Butter, cooking oils, ghee, lard, margarine, reduced and low-fat spreads
- Cheese, eggs

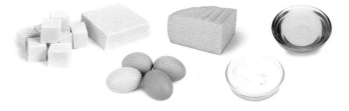

ⵊ RICE, QUINOA, & OTHER GLUTEN-FREE GRAINS AND FLOURS

All grains, flours, and flour mixes labelled "gluten-free", including: amaranth, buckwheat, cassava, chestnut flour, chickpea flour, corn (maize), corn starch, gram flour, millet, mustard flour, polenta (cornmeal), potato flour, potato starch, oats , quinoa, rice, rice bran, rice flour, sago, sorghum, soya flour, tapioc, tapioca starch, teff, and urad flour.

GOODBYE TO PASTA, BREAD, CAKES, PASTRY, AND BISCUITS?

As more people follow a gluten-free diet, the food industry has responded to their needs by developing an expanding range of gluten-free products, including cakes, biscuits, pasta, ready-made pastry, and bread. Of course, there's no need to rely on ready-made products: you can use commercial gluten-free flour blends – or blend your own – to bake at home, adapt favourite recipes, and try new ones. Some shop-bought bakes are better than others, but none can match the taste of home-made.

GLUTEN FREE ON THE GO

EATING AT A RESTAURANT

Eating out may seem a little daunting when you first start on a gluten-free diet. Follow a few simple ground rules, however, and there is absolutely no reason why you can't enjoy dining out at restaurants just as much as before.

6 TIPS FOR DINING OUT

1 Ask around If you have joined a coeliac group, ask local members if they can recommend restaurants in your area that cater for gluten-free diets.

2 Look online Many online review sites now list gluten-free restaurants. You will also often find menus published online to check ahead.

3 Get in touch Contact the restaurant at least 24 hours before you intend to visit, to check whether they are properly set up for gluten-free cooking.

4 Don't be shy Emphasize to the restaurant just how important it is for you to remain gluten free. Try to talk to the chef to confirm what's in each dish.

5 Check their set-up Explain that even a tiny amount of gluten flour is harmful and ask if they have kitchen systems to guard against cross contamination.

6 BYO If you want to bring your own gluten-free bread to eat at the start of the meal, do ask ahead and confirm again with the waiter when you arrive.

HOW DO I STAY GLUTEN FREE TRAVELLING ABROAD?

If you have joined a coeliac organization, it should be able to provide you with country-specific leaflets about gluten-free eating abroad, including language translations with useful phrases to help when you are dining out. It's always worth packing emergency gluten-free snacks, however, and items such as pasta, bread, and toaster bags in your suitcase.

WHAT ABOUT TAKEAWAYS?

At chip shops and burger outlets you need to be certain everything you ask for is cooked in fresh oil. Prepared meats are usually not suitable and if they use frozen chips these are often coated in flour. Many dishes from Indian takeaways will be fine to eat, provided they use fresh ingredients and whole spices. Watch out for soy sauce in Chinese takeaways.

GLUTEN-FREE PACKED LUNCH

A growing number of cafés are beginning to offer gluten-free choices, but they are few and far between and you may pay extra for the privilege. Packing your own lunch and snacks is often the best option, and providing your child with a packed lunch will help reassure you that they are eating well and staying gluten free away from home.

NUTS
A handful of nuts provide healthy fats and protein. Avoid roasted nuts, which can contain flour.

DRIED FRUIT
Ready-to-eat dried fruit, such as apricots, are a good source of dietary fibre, but do contain concentrated sugars, so go easy.

FRESH FRUIT
An apple or other piece of fresh fruit is the perfect gluten-free and healthy choice for snacking.

BREAKFAST BARS
Granola-type bars made with oats and crispy rice are great for breakfast on the go or a mid-morning snack.

SANDWICH
Baking your own bread for sandwiches will make eating them a treat, not a chore. Bake a few loaves at a time and freeze them for several weeks' supply.

HOME-MADE SWEET TREATS
Treat yourself to a home-made biscuit or slice of cake a couple of times a week: teabreads are a healthier, low-fat option.

6 SNACKING TIPS FOR KIDS

1 **Send them prepared** Make sure you always send your kids off with plenty of gluten-free snacks in case there is nothing else suitable to eat.

2 **Offer variety** Children can quickly get bored of eating the same snacks, so try to provide them with a changing menu across the week.

3 **Go natural** If your child is concerned about feeling different, include naturally gluten-free snacks like cheese portions, sesame bars, popcorn, and smoothies.

4 **Make at home** Cakes and biscuits are easy and fun for children to bake at home, and they will be excited to eat a snack they've made themselves.

5 **Don't spoil the party** Secretly bring some gluten-free snacks and treats when you drop off your child at a party, so they don't miss out on a party bag.

6 **Teach independence** Make sure older children know what to look for on the ingredients list, so they can choose suitable snacks for themselves.

GLUTEN-FREE GRAINS

A trip to a good health food shop or a large, well-stocked supermarket will reveal a huge range of gluten-free grains that are nutritious, tasty, and extremely versatile. Exploring the many non-gluten grains can transform going gluten free into an opportunity to discover a new world of tastes and textures.

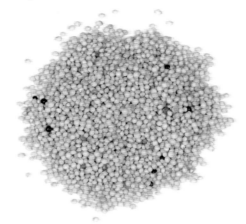

« AMARANTH
Amaranthus spp.

A seed rather than true grain, amaranth is rich in protein and provides useful amounts of calcium, iron, and magnesium, with more fibre than other gluten-free grains. Amaranth has a slightly peppery, nutty flavour and sticky texture. It can be cooked as a cereal, ground into flour, popped like popcorn, sprouted, or toasted. The seeds can be added to stir-fries, soups, and stews as a thickening agent.

QUINOA »
Chenopodium quinoa

Sacred to the Incas, quinoa has been cultivated in South America since 3,000 BC. It is extremely high in protein and provides useful amounts of phosphorus, calcium, iron, vitamin E, and B vitamins, as well as fibre. With a delicious nutty flavour and pleasant texture, quinoa can be boiled and used instead of rice for salads or pilafs, to make stuffings, as an accompaniment to stews, or added to breakfast cereals. It is also available as flour.

« BUCKWHEAT
Fagopyrum esculentum

Despite the name, buckwheat is not related to wheat and does not contain gluten: it is a seed from a plant that is a relative of rhubarb. Buckwheat groats are buckwheat kernels stripped of their inedible outer coating and then crushed into smaller pieces. Unprocessed groats are slightly bitter, so before you cook them it's a good idea to toast them in oil for a few minutes; this removes the bitterness and brings out a pleasant, nutty flavour. Buckwheat groats can be used as an alternative to couscous.

⚹ OATS
Avena sativa

Compared to other cereals, oats contain higher levels of both protein and fat. They also provide useful amounts of B vitamins and the minerals calcium, magnesium, iron, and zinc. Oats are rich in beta glucan, a type of soluble fibre that can help to reduce high blood cholesterol levels. Whole oats or oat groats take 1¼ hours to cook, retaining their shape but turning creamy. They make a delicious addition to meat or vegetable stews, and precooked oats can be baked into coarse-grain bread doughs.

SAGO »
Metroxylon sagu

Extracted from the spongy centre of tropical palm stems grown in Papua New Guinea and Southeast Asia, sago is virtually pure carbohydrate and offers very little protein, vitamins, minerals, or fibre. Sago pearls are small grains similar to tapioca and can be used to make desserts. Sago can also be ground into flour, which can be used to make pancakes, baked goods, noodles, or for thickening stews or gravies.

⌃ KASHA
Fagopyrum esculentum

Kasha, not to be confused with kamut, a variety of wheat, is the Russian name for a wholegrain cereal made from roasted whole buckwheat groats. Toasting the groats helps to remove buckwheat's natural bitterness and to bring out a sweeter, nuttier flavour. They come whole or crushed into a coarse, medium, or fine grain.

« MILLET
Pennisetum glaucum

Millet is a small, round, yellow grain containing useful amounts of protein, vitamins, minerals, and fibre. A staple food in many parts of Africa and Asia, where it is eaten as a porridge or used to make bread, it has a rather mild flavour and can be used in breakfast cereals or for dishes such as pilaf. It can be ground and made into flour for Indian-style breads like rotis.

⌄ WILD RICE
Zizania spp.

Wild rice is not actually rice but the seeds of freshwater grass. It contains twice as much protein as rice, and higher levels of B vitamins, zinc, iron, and fibre. The long, thin black seeds have a distinctive nutty, slightly woody flavour, and a chewy texture. It can be cooked and served in the same way as ordinary rice, although it takes about 10 minutes longer to cook. Try mixing half and half with basmati rice.

⌃ RICE
Oryza sativa

There are many different varieties of rice including basmati, sticky, red, brown, and risotto, all of which are gluten free. As well as served plain as an accompaniment, rice can be used to make sweet and savoury dishes such as pilaf, risotto, and rice pudding. It can also be made into rice flour, noodles, pancakes, spring roll wrappers, and rice cakes. Brown rice is a wholegrain cereal and contains more vitamins, minerals, and fibre than refined white rice, from which the germ and bran are removed.

GLUTEN-FREE FLOURS

Wheat is not the only flour. Around the world, and often for thousands of years, people have been producing and using flours from an array of non-wheat grains, seeds, nuts, beans, and vegetables. Learn how to cook with them, get to know their distinctive qualities, and create your favourite blends for baking.

« CORNMEAL FLOUR

Cornmeal flour is made from sweetcorn kernels that have been dried, soaked in lime water, washed, and ground into a coarse flour. Stoneground cornmeal retains some of the bran and germ of the dried kernels that standard milling removes, and thus tends to have a better flavour and nutrient value. Cornmeal flour is a good ingredient to use as a crumb coating for fried foods and in addition can be used to make corn tortillas (try to source the authentic Mexican variety *masa harina*), pancakes, muffins, and corn bread. Popcorn is made from a special hard variety of corn kernel and is a good gluten-free snack.

CORNFLOUR »

Not to be confused with cornmeal, cornflour is the pure starch extracted from corn kernels. Almost tasteless and easily blended with liquids without the need for additional fat, the fine white powder is commonly used as a thickener for sauces but can be mixed with other flours for baking.

⌃ CORNMEAL (COARSE)

Coarsely ground cornmeal, also known as polenta, can be cooked as a savoury accompaniment, either boiled to give a "porridge" (wet polenta) or left to set then cut into slabs and fried or grilled. Coarse cornmeal can also be used in conjunction with other flours in baked goods, but instant or quick-cook varieties have a grittier, crunchy texture that is less appealing in cakes.

« BUCKWHEAT FLOUR

Buckwheat is higher in protein than other gluten-free flours and has a strong, slightly sweet taste and speckled appearance. Japanese soba noodles are traditionally made with buckwheat flour and it is also good for making pancakes, blinis, and pasta.

TEFF FLOUR »

High in protein and fibre, and with a slightly sweet, nutty flavour, teff flour is made from the seeds of a grass native to Ethiopia. The flour can be used in combination with other gluten-free flours in baking. The whole seeds can be used to make porridge, added to soups or stews, or served as an accompaniment instead of rice, millet, or bulgur wheat. Teff also provides useful amounts of iron, calcium, magnesium, and zinc.

⌃ OATMEAL

Oatmeal is produced by milling the hulled whole oats. The grains are milled to different levels of fineness: coarse oatmeal can be used for stuffings, thickening soups and stews, and sprinkling in place of breadcrumbs over dishes to be gratinéed; medium oatmeal is the most versatile for baking and gives an even coating to fried fish; fine oatmeal can be worked to a smooth texture suitable for pancakes, pastry, and gravies. Always choose oatmeals marked gluten-free as they can be contaminated in the milling process.

« TAPIOCA FLOUR

Low in protein and other nutrients, tapioca flour is almost pure starch and largely flavourless. It can be used by itself to make puddings and to thicken soups or sauces, or blended with other gluten-free flours for baking. Tapioca also makes a crisp, golden crust when used as a batter or "bread" coating for fried food.

⌄ CHESTNUT FLOUR

Made from the ground whole nuts, chestnut flour is high in fibre, healthy fats, and protein, and contributes additional texture, moisture, and a slightly sweet flavour to cakes and biscuits. Chestnut flour is also good for making pancakes.

⌃ ALMOND FLOUR

Made by grinding blanched almonds, almond flour is high in fibre, healthy fats, and protein, and provides good amounts of calcium. Use it in gluten-free baking to add extra flavour, moisture, and texture, and for improving nutritional value.

« SOY FLOUR

Soy flour is made from ground soybeans and comes in defatted, low fat, and full-fat varieties. An excellent source of protein and B vitamins, it has a strong "beany" flavour and is best used in combination with other flours.

^ WHITE RICE FLOUR

White rice flour has a mild flavour and can be used as a sauce thickener in the same way as cornflour: simply mix first with cold water before adding to the sauce and cooking until thickened. It is also used, particularly in Asian cooking, to make dumplings, pancakes, cakes, and sweets. "Ground rice" is also made from white rice and has a slightly grittier texture that helps give a crispy finish to pastries and biscuits.

POTATO FLOUR »

Also called potato starch or farina, potato flour helps retain moisture and gives a fine, light texture to baked goods. It also makes an excellent thickening agent. Like cornflour and tapioca, potato flour is high in refined carbohydrates and low in fibre and nutrients.

¥ SORGHUM FLOUR

Milled from grains of sorghum, a cereal crop, sorghum flour is a high-protein flour with a smooth texture and bland taste. It is best mixed in small proportions with other gluten-free flours to provide extra protein.

^ BROWN RICE FLOUR

Brown rice flour can be used in the same way as white rice flour but it has a more grainy texture and stronger, nutty flavour that helps to provide a "wholemeal" taste and texture when used in flour blends for baking.

⌄ URAD DAL FLOUR

Milled from urad beans, urad dal flour is a protein-rich staple of South Indian cooking where it is used to make dosas, uttapams, idli, and papadums. The flour can also be used in conjunction with other flours in flatbreads, as a thickener, and added to soups and purées for additional protein.

⌃ CHICKPEA FLOUR

Also known as gram or besan flour, chickpea flour is high in protein and fibre, and has a distinctive "beany" flavour. It is widely used in Indian cuisine to make the batter for bhajis and pakoras, and in papadums and breads. Chickpea flour is also useful for thickening soups and sauces, but should be mixed with other flours for general baking.

Other useful ingredients

Going gluten free is a great opportunity for many people to bake at home for the first time. As well as raising agents common to all baking, a gluten-free baker needs extra ingredients to help replace the elastic quality of gluten-containing flours.

⌄ GLUTEN-FREE BAKING POWDER

Used in cake baking, once activated by the liquid in a cake mix, baking powder undergoes a chemical reaction that produces carbon dioxide gas to help the cake rise.

⌄ GLUTEN-FREE BICARBONATE OF SODA

Bicarbonate of soda is similar to baking powder but requires the addition of the natural acid in ingredients such as buttermilk or yogurt to produce the same chemical reaction.

⌄ YEAST

Yeast is a living micro-organism, which, when added to dough, creates the carbon dioxide that causes bread to rise. Available fresh or dried, fast-action dried yeast is probably the most useful for novice bakers.

⌄ XANTHAN GUM

Xanthan gum helps gluten-free doughs to bind together and adds some elasticity, making bread less crumbly and pastry easier to roll and handle. Buy it online, in health food shops, or large supermarkets. Guar gum has similar properties but can be more difficult to source.

⌄ ARROWROOT

A white starch made from the root of a tropical herb, arrowroot helps to bind ingredients together, adding body and texture to baked goods. It is also useful as a clear thickener for soups and sauces.

MAKING PASTA

Making your own pasta is time-consuming but hugely rewarding, and the results are a world apart from the dried gluten-free pasta available to buy. If pasta is your passion, then, it is well worth investing in a pasta machine (or dusting off the one you've never used!). Set aside time to make a large batch and freeze in individual portions; fresh pasta freezes well and can be cooked straight from frozen.

MAKES 350G (12OZ)
PREP 40 MINS
COOK 3-4 MINS

85g (3oz) tapioca flour
85g (3oz) cornflour
3 tbsp potato flour
3 tsp xanthan gum
½ tsp salt
3 eggs
2 tbsp olive oil
gluten-free plain flour,
    for dusting

SPECIAL EQUIPMENT
pasta machine with
    tagliatelle attachment

FRESH EGG PASTA

Here the pasta dough is formed into tagliatelle. Other standard cutter attachments include spaghetti and fettuccine, but the rolled pasta can be formed into any shape or left flat for lasagne sheets and ravioli. If not using immediately, place the pasta on trays dusted with cornmeal, cover with cling film or a tea towel, and leave for up to 4 hours.

1 Sift the flours, xanthan, and salt into a large bowl. In another bowl, beat together the eggs and oil. Make a well in the centre of the flours, then pour in the egg and oil mix.

2 Use a palette knife or round-bladed table knife to draw the flour into the liquid. Mix until it starts to bind, then finally bring it together with your hands to form a dough.

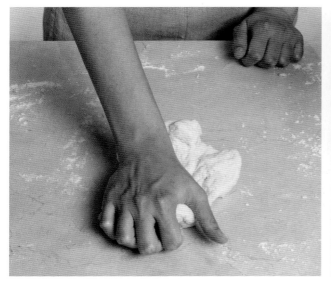

3 Transfer the dough to a lightly floured surface and knead gently until it becomes smooth. Wrap tightly in cling film and leave to rest for 10 minutes. Unwrap the dough and divide it into 4 equal pieces.

4 Take one of the pieces of dough and, using a rolling pin, roll it out to a long strip, about 12cm (5in) wide and 5mm (¼in) thick. Set aside and cover with a damp, clean tea towel, as you repeat the process with the remaining dough.

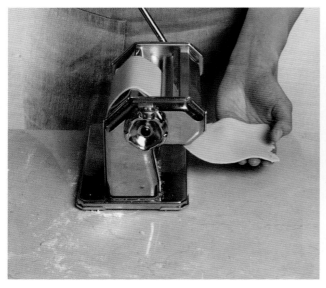

5 Dusting well with more flour, pass each strip of dough through a pasta machine 4 times. Adjust the dial by a stop each time until the pasta is really thin; don't worry if a few holes appear. Dust and set aside each sheet.

6 Attach the cutter and pass the flour-dusted strips through the machine to form the tagliatelle. To cook, bring a large pan of water to a rolling boil, add the pasta, and cook for 3–4 minutes; the pasta should still have some "bite".

MAKING PASTRY

Though a little more delicate to handle than traditional pastry, with practice you will soon master the art of gluten-free pastry and the results are well worth the effort. The addition of egg and xanthan gum helps the dough to bind, making it easier to roll out and giving the cooked pastry a crisp, flaky consistency that is almost indistinguishable from pastry made with wheat flour.

MAKES 400G (14OZ)
ENOUGH FOR A
MEDIUM TART CASE
PREP 20 MINS
COOK 20 MINS
PLUS CHILLING

225g (8oz) gluten-free plain flour, plus extra for dusting
1 tsp xanthan gum
pinch of salt
100g (3½oz) cold butter, cubed
1 egg, beaten

SPECIAL EQUIPMENT
23cm (9in) round tart tin, ceramic baking beans (optional, see step 5)

VARIATION
Sweet shortcrust pastry
Add 2 tbsp icing sugar with the flour before blending into crumbs. After blind baking, brush the pastry case with egg wash from 1 egg, beaten, and bake for a further 5 minutes to crisp up.

SHORTCRUST PASTRY

The pastry dough is here used to "blind" bake a case for tarts and quiches, but it is also perfect for making single and double crust pies and tartes Tatin. If you get a few cracks and holes as you lift the pastry and line the tin, simply patch them up with excess pastry and "glue" together with a little water to seal.

1 Preheat the oven to 200°C (400°F/Gas 6). Sift the flour, xanthan, and salt into a bowl and mix. Add the butter and rub it in with your fingertips until the mixture forms crumbs. Alternatively, you can do this by pulsing the mixture in a food processor.

2 Add the egg and mix it in with a palette knife or round-bladed table knife. Gradually add 1–2 tablespoons cold water, a few drops at a time, mixing after each addition. Keep adding water and mixing until it just comes together to form a dough.

3 Transfer the dough to a floured surface and briefly and lightly knead until smooth. Wrap in cling film and chill in the fridge for 10 minutes. Roll out the pastry on a lightly floured surface until it is about 5mm (¼in) thick and large enough to fill the tin.

4 Carefully wrap the pastry around the rolling pin, lift over the tin, and unroll the pastry. To line the tin, gently press the pastry into the base and sides, pressing it into the flutes if you are using a fluted tin. Trim the edges, repair any holes, and prick the base with a fork.

5 Line the pastry with baking parchment and weigh down the parchment with ceramic baking beans (or you can use ordinary dried beans, such as haricots). Place on a baking sheet and bake in the preheated oven for 15 minutes.

6 Remove the tart from the oven and carefully lift out the parchment and beans. Return to the oven for another 5 minutes to crisp up, then add the filling of your choice and bake as per recipe instructions.

ROUGH PUFF PASTRY

115g (4oz) butter, wrapped
in foil and frozen for
1 hour until hard
175g (6oz) gluten-free plain
flour, plus extra for dusting
large pinch of salt
1 tsp xanthan gum

1 Sift the flour, xanthan, and salt into a large bowl. Unwrap the butter and, still holding it in the foil (this stops the heat of your hand melting it), coarsely grate it into the flour.

2 Stir the butter and flour until well mixed. Gradually add 120ml (4fl oz) ice-cold water, stirring with a palette knife or round-bladed table knife until it forms a dough.

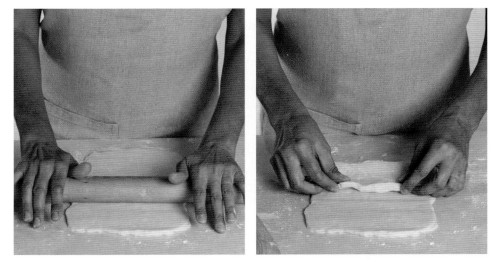

3 On a lighty floured surface, briefly knead the dough into a ball, then wrap in cling film and chill in the fridge for 10 minutes. Roll out the pastry to a rectangle 20 x 35cm (8 x 14in).

4 Mentally divide the pastry into thirds, or you could lightly score it with the back of a knife. Fold the bottom third of the pastry up over the middle third.

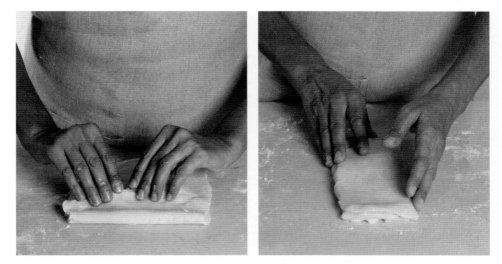

5 Now take the top third of the pastry and fold it down over the bottom third. Lightly press together the edges to seal the "parcel".

6 Give the dough a quarter turn. Roll out again and fold as before, wrap in cling film, and chill in the fridge for at least 20 minutes.

HOT WATER CRUST

MAKES 500G (1LB 2OZ)
PREP   20 MINS

350g (12oz) gluten-free plain
  flour, plus extra for dusting
2 tsp xanthan gum
1 tsp salt
3 tbsp milk
100g (3½oz) lard or white
  vegetable fat
1 egg

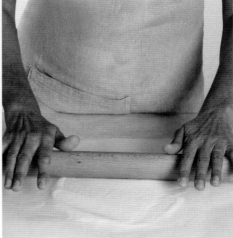

1 Sift the flour, xanthan, and salt into a large bowl. Gently heat 250ml (8fl oz) water with the milk and lard until just boiling. Pour the hot liquid into the flour and quickly beat with a wooden spoon until it forms a dough.

2 Turn the dough out onto a lightly floured surface and knead gently until smooth. This pastry can be sticky and difficult to handle, and when rolling out you may find it easier to roll between sheets of baking parchment.

BREAD FLOUR BLENDS
Makes 700g (1lb 8½oz)

White bread flour	Brown bread flour
450g (1lb) white rice flour	450g (1lb) brown rice flour
115g (4oz) potato flour	115g (4oz) potato flour
60g (2oz) tapioca flour	60g (2oz) tapioca flour
60g (2oz) cornflour	60g (2oz) cornflour
4 tsp xanthan gum	4 tsp xanthan gum

RECIPES

The recipes in this book have been selected, devised, and tested to provide delicious gluten-free replacements to many favourite dishes normally made with gluten-containing grains, or where the shop- bought variety often include added gluten. We have also sought to offer a wide range of options for dishes that use ingredients from non-gluten grains, and some gluten-free versions of takeaway favourites.

A "Guidelines per serving" chart is provided for each recipe, weighted according to the type of meal and the proportion of daily intake you should be getting from that meal. This tells you

CALORIES

SATURATED FAT

SALT

at a glance whether the recipe is high (3 dots), medium (2 dots), or low (1 dot) in calories, saturated fat, and salt – three key areas to watch for a healthy diet. If you choose a recipe that is high in any of these areas, aim to choose dishes that are medium or low in those areas for the rest of the day. Each recipe also has a "Statistics per serving" breakdown of the number of calories and amount of protein, fat, carbohydrate, sugar, fibre, and salt in the dish. So if you really need to crunch the numbers, you can ensure you're getting the exact balance.

Flours and other ingredients made from non-gluten grains, such as rice noodles and cornmeal, are assumed to be gluten free in the ingredients lists, but always check the label as there can be a risk of contamination with gluten grains at the milling stage.

GRANOLA WITH APPLE CRISPS

SERVES 8   **PREP** 20 MINS   **COOK** 1½–2 HOURS

This granola is on the right side of sweetness and will give you bags of energy at the start of the day.

4–6 dessert apples, cored
  and very thinly sliced into rings
juice of 1 lemon
1 tsp demerara sugar
3 tsp ground cinnamon
200g (7oz) buckwheat flakes
200g (7oz) rice flakes

drizzle of clear honey or maple syrup
3 tbsp sunflower oil
200g (7oz) blanched almonds
300g (10oz) dried apricots,
  roughly chopped
100g (3½oz) dried cranberries
milk and natural yogurt, to serve

1 For the apple crisps, preheat the oven to 150°C (300°F/Gas 2). Toss the apples in lemon juice and arrange them in a single layer on baking sheets lined with baking parchment. Sprinkle with the sugar and 1 teaspoon of the cinnamon and put in the oven. Leave for about 1–1½ hours, keeping an eye on them and turning them halfway through. Turn the oven down to 140°C (275°F/Gas 1) if they begin to colour too much. Remove and spread on clean parchment to dry out. If you have time, leave them in the oven overnight, after switching off the heat, to crisp up some more.

2 Set the oven temperature to 180°C (350°F/Gas 4). Place the buckwheat flakes, rice flakes, and the remaining cinnamon in a large bowl (you can substitute other gluten-free grains, such as quinoa flakes or puffs, millet flakes, or soya flakes). Mix the honey or maple syrup with the oil, pour it over the grain mixture, and toss until all the flakes are well coated. Tip out onto a baking tray and bake for 10 minutes or until golden. Stir well, add the almonds, and cook for a further 20 minutes or until the nuts are lightly toasted. Remove from the oven, stir in the dried fruit, and leave to cool. Serve with the apple crisps, milk, and a dollop of natural yogurt.

COOK'S TIP
You can also double up the quantities for the granola and apple crisps and store them in separate airtight containers for up to 3 weeks.

STATISTICS PER SERVING

Energy 446kcals/1868kJ

Protein 8.5g

Fat 12.4g
Saturated fat 1.1g

Carbohydrate 64.2g
Sugar 27g

Fibre 7.4g

Salt trace

● ● ● CALORIES

● ● ○ SATURATED FAT

● ○ ○ SALT

BREAKFAST BERRY BARS

SERVES 8   **PREP** 10 MINS   **COOK** 30-35 MIN

So easy to make, these fruit-packed bars are ready to grab for a breakfast on the go!

oil, for greasing
397g can sweetened condensed milk
300g (10oz) mixed dried berries,
  such as cranberries, blueberries,
  and sour cherries
250g (9oz) rolled oats

50g (1¾oz) crispy rice
30g (1oz) sunflower seeds
30g (1oz) pumpkin seeds

SPECIAL EQUIPMENT 23 x 33cm
  (9 x 13in) rectangular baking tin

1 Preheat the oven to 160°C (325°F/Gas 3). Lightly oil the baking tray.

2 Gently heat the condensed milk in a large, heavy pan and slowly bring to the boil. Remove it from the heat, then tip in the fruit, oats, crispy rice, and seeds. Mix well with a wooden spoon.

3 Tip into the prepared tin, then level the surface with the back of a wetted spoon. Bake for 30–35 minutes or until pale golden.

4 Remove from the oven, cool in the tin for 5 minutes, and cut into 16 bars. Transfer the bars to a wire rack to cool completely. Store in an airtight container for up to 1 week.

STATISTICS PER SERVING

Energy 476kcals/2000kJ

Protein 11g

Fat 12g

Saturated fat 4g

Carbohydrate 80g

Sugar 44g

Fibre 7g

Salt 0.3g

COOK'S TIP
Tailor these to suit your personal taste: chopped dried apricots, sultanas, or raisins can be used instead of the berries, just keep the quantity the same; and try using the same quantity of chopped hazelnuts in place of the seeds.

● ● ● CALORIES

● ● ● SATURATED FAT

● ○ ○ SALT

MUESLI WITH TOASTED COCONUT

SERVES 6   **PREP** 15 MINS   **COOK** 5 MINS

The sticky dates add a toffee-flavoured sweetness to this super-healthy mix of flakes, seeds, fruits, and nuts.

75g (2½oz) rice flakes
75g (2½oz) buckwheat flakes
75g (2½oz) milled linseed
175g (6oz) soft pitted dates, chopped
75g (2½oz) dried sour cherries
125g (4½oz) Brazil nuts,
  roughly chopped

50g (1¾oz) sunflower seeds
100g (3½oz) desiccated coconut
milk, Greek yogurt, and fresh seasonal
  fruit of your choice, to serve

1 Place the flakes, linseed, dates, cherries, Brazil nuts, and sunflower seeds in a large bowl and mix.

2 Place the desiccated coconut in a frying pan and dry fry gently for a few minutes until golden, stirring it around the pan so it doesn't burn.

3 Divide the muesli between 6 individual serving bowls, then sprinkle with the coconut. Pour over enough milk for serving and top with Greek yogurt and fresh fruit, if desired.

COOK'S TIP
The quantities can easily be scaled up and the muesli stored in an airtight container for up to 3 weeks. If storing, allow the coconut to cool before stirring it into the mix.

STATISTICS PER SERVING

Energy 557kcals/2322kJ

Protein 12g

Fat 34g
Saturated fat 14g

Carbohydrate 49g
Sugar 29g

Fibre 10g

Salt trace

« Dried sour cherries
These have a marvellously tart, yet fruity flavour. As well as in muesli, try them on their own as a snack or use in baking. Store in an airtight container for up to 6 months.

PORRIDGE WITH FRUIT COMPOTE

SERVES 6   **PREP** 10 MINS   **COOK** 20 MINS

Classic porridge, served with aniseed-infused fruits, is a real treat for breakfast. For a less indulgent porridge, replace the cream with more milk.

200g (7oz) rolled oats
750ml (1¼ pints) milk, plus extra
  if needed
250ml (9fl oz) single cream

For the compote
200g (7oz) soft pitted prunes
75g (2½oz) sour cherries
300ml (10fl oz) fresh orange juice
1 star anise

1 First prepare the compote. Place the prunes and cherries in a pan and pour over the orange juice, add the star anise, bring to the boil, then reduce the heat and simmer gently for 15 minutes. Set aside to steep.

2 Meanwhile, place the oats in a pan. Add two-thirds of the milk and stir well so it is all incorporated. Bring slowly to the boil, stirring continuously, until the milk has been absorbed by the oats. Gradually stir in the remaining milk and the cream, bring back to the boil, and simmer gently, stirring, for 10–15 minutes or until thick and creamy. Add more milk, if needed.

3 Drain the dried fruit, reserving the liquid, and remove the star anise. Ladle the porridge into deep bowls and top with the drained fruit and a little of the reserved juice.

NUTRiENT BOOST
Prunes are rich in fibre, good for digestion and controlling blood cholesterol.

VARIATIONS
Try flavouring the porridge with some warming cinnamon spice: add 1 cinnamon stick and 2 teaspoons ground cinnamon to the oats along with the milk. When it's ready, remove the stick and serve with a sprinkle of cinnamon and a swirl of cream. The spice gives the porridge a sweet flavour, so there is no need to add sugar. You can also swap the fruits with dried apricots and sultanas, or figs and cranberries.

COOK'S TIP
You can store the fruit compote in an airtight container in the fridge for up to 1 week.

GUIDELINES PER SERVING

●●● CALORIES

●●● SATURATED FAT

●○○ SALT

STATISTICS PER SERVING

Energy 403kcals/1692kJ

Protein 11g

Fat 16g
Saturated fat 8g

Carbohydrate 54g
Sugar 31g

Fibre 7g

Salt 0.3g

BUTTERMILK PANCAKES

SERVES 4   **PREP** 5 MINS   **COOK** 10 MINS   **FREEZE** 6 MONTHS

A stack of pancakes served with maple syrup and fresh fruit is hard to beat for a special family breakfast. Heat the pancakes slowly so that they cook in the middle.

85g (3oz) rice flour
1 tsp xanthan gum
1 tbsp caster sugar
1½ tsp gluten-free baking powder
pinch of salt
150ml (5fl oz) buttermilk

4 tbsp milk
2 large eggs, separated
a few drops of vanilla extract
vegetable oil, for frying
maple syrup and fresh berries,
   to serve

1 Sift the flour, xanthan, sugar, baking powder, and salt together into a bowl. Add the buttermilk, milk, egg yolks, and vanilla, and beat well.

2 In a clean bowl, whisk the egg whites with an electric whisk until they are stiff. Stir a good spoonful of egg white into the batter mix to loosen it, then gently fold in the remainder.

3 Heat a large, heavy frying pan over a medium-high heat, add a few drops of oil, and wipe it around the pan with a piece of kitchen paper. Drop 4 separate heaped dessertspoons of batter into the hot pan to make 4 pancakes, leaving plenty of space between them; they should spread to be about 8cm (3¼in) wide. Cook them over a low heat for about 2–3 minutes until the base is golden, then flip them over and cook for a further 2 minutes.

4 Once cooked, wrap the pancakes in a clean tea towel to keep them warm. Repeat to make 8 pancakes in total. Serve warm, drizzled with maple syrup and with a handful of fresh berries scattered on top.

STATISTICS PER SERVING

Energy 218kcals/912kJ

Protein 8g

Fat 10g
Saturated fat 2g

Carbohydrate 22g
Sugar 6g

Fibre 0.6g

Salt 1g

⬤⬤⬤⬤ CALORIES

⬤⬤⬤ SATURATED FAT

⬤⬤◯ SALT

EGGS BENEDICT

SERVES 4   **PREP** 20 MINS   **COOK** 35 MINS   **FREEZE** 3 MONTHS
PLUS RISING

If you prefer white muffins, use the gluten-free white bread flour blend on page 24 and add two tablespoons caster sugar.

450g (1lb) gluten-free brown bread
  flour blend (see page 24), plus extra
  for dusting
2 tsp fast-action dried yeast
1 tsp xanthan gum
salt and freshly ground black pepper
300ml (10fl oz) milk

90g (3oz) unsalted butter, plus extra
2 tbsp black treacle
5 eggs, plus 2 egg yolks
3 tbsp white wine vinegar

SPECIAL EQUIPMENT 7.5cm (3in) round
  metal cutter, griddle pan

1 Sift the flour, yeast, xanthan, and a pinch of salt into a large bowl and stir to combine. Warm the milk to lukewarm, add 15g (½oz) butter, the treacle, and 1 egg, and whisk with a fork. Make a well in the centre of the dry ingredients, add the wet ingredients, and mix. Turn onto a lightly floured surface and knead for 5 minutes until smooth. Roll out the dough 2cm (¾in) thick and cut out 8 rounds. Transfer to a floured baking sheet, cover with oiled cling film, and leave somewhere warm for 1 hour until doubled.

2 Heat a large, heavy frying pan or flat griddle. Add the muffins, making sure they don't touch each other, and cook over a medium heat for 6–7 minutes or until the bases are golden. Turn over, place a baking sheet on top of the pan to intensify the heat, and cook for 7–8 minutes until golden.

3 To poach the eggs, place a frying pan over a low heat and add boiling water to a depth of 2.5cm (1in). Carefully break 4 eggs, one at a time, into the water and let them barely simmer, for 1 minute. Remove the pan from the heat and set aside for 10 minutes to finish poaching.

4 For the hollandaise sauce, simmer the vinegar in a small pan until reduced by half. Pour into a heatproof bowl with the egg yolks and place over a pan of gently simmering water. Melt 75g (2½oz) butter, gradually add it to the bowl, and whisk continuously with a balloon whisk until a smooth, thick sauce forms. Remove from the heat and season. Split and butter the muffins, top each half with an egg, and pour over the sauce.

STATISTICS PER SERVING

Energy 753kcals/3167kJ

Protein 28g

Fat 38g

Saturated fat 19g

Carbohydrate 75g

Sugar 11g

Fibre 13.5g

Salt 0.8g

MASALA DOSA

SERVES 6　　**PREP** 20 MINS　　**COOK** 40-50 MINS　　**FREEZE** 1 MONTH
PLUS SOAKING

These spicy vegan pancakes, made from ground lentils and rice, are traditionally served for breakfast in southern India.

175g (6oz) basmati rice
60g (2oz) urad dal
1 tsp fenugreek seeds
salt
vegetable oil, for frying

For the potato filling
2 tbsp vegetable oil
1 onion, finely chopped
1 green chilli, deseeded and chopped
1 garlic clove, finely chopped
2.5cm (1in) piece of fresh root ginger, grated

2 tsp black mustard seeds
¼ tsp turmeric
6 dried curry leaves
450g (1lb) potatoes, cubed
zest and juice of ½ lemon
2 tbsp finely chopped fresh coriander

For the dipping sauce
30g (1oz) fresh coriander
1 small tomato
½ green chilli, deseeded
juice of 1 lemon
½ tsp caster sugar

1 Place the rice, dal, and fenugreek seeds in a large bowl, cover with cold water, and soak for 6–8 hours or overnight. Drain and coarsely grind in a food processor with a pinch of salt. Add 300ml (10fl oz) cold water and process to a smooth batter the consistency of thin cream.

2 For the spicy potato filling, heat the oil in a medium pan and fry the onion for 4 minutes or until soft. Add the chilli, garlic, ginger, mustard seeds, turmeric, and curry leaves and cook for 30 seconds or until the mustard seeds start to pop. Add the potatoes, lemon zest and juice, a good pinch of salt, and 250ml (8fl oz) water. Bring to the boil, cover, and simmer for 15–20 minutes until tender. Remove the lid and simmer until soft and breaking up. Stir in the coriander and keep warm. For the sauce, place all the ingredients with a pinch of salt in a food processor and whizz to a rough paste.

3 Heat 1 teaspoon oil in a small frying pan. Cover the pan with a ladleful of batter and cook over medium heat for 2–3 minutes. Flip and cook for another 1–2 minutes. Keep warm. Repeat to make 5 pancakes. Divide the potato filling between the pancakes, fold over, and serve with the sauce.

STATISTICS PER SERVING

Energy 250kcals/1049kJ

Protein 6.5g

Fat 6g
Saturated fat 0.7g

Carbohydrate 40g
Sugar 2.3g

Fibre 3g

Salt 0.3g

MINESTRONE SOUP

SERVES 8   **PREP** 40 MINS   **COOK** 1¾–2¼ HOURS   **FREEZE** 3 MONTHS

This soup can use up a glut of seasonal vegetables, simply change them depending on the time of the year.

NUTRIENT BOOST
Canned beans and pulses are an excellent source of soluble fibre.

1 ham knuckle or "hock", or 1 pack
   of bacon, roughly chopped
1 tbsp olive oil
1 medium onion, finely chopped
2 bay leaves
3 large carrots, diced
1 fennel bulb, finely chopped
2 garlic cloves, finely chopped
freshly ground black pepper
4 large ripe tomatoes, chopped
leaves from a few thyme sprigs
pinch of freshly grated nutmeg
400g can chickpeas, drained
   and rinsed

400g can cannellini or butter beans,
   drained and rinsed
100g (3½oz) broad beans, fresh
   or defrosted, shelled weight
100g (3½oz) peas, fresh or defrosted,
   shelled weight
200g (7oz) small gluten-free
   pasta shapes (shop-bought or
   see pages 18-19)
100g (3½oz) spinach

1 Put the ham pieces in a large pan and add enough cold water to nearly fill the pan. Bring to the boil, reduce to a medium-low heat, partially cover the pan with a lid, and cook for 1–1½ hours or until the ham begins to soften. Strain the stock, reserving the bones and meat. Strain the stock again, through a fine sieve, into a measuring jug; you will need 1.2 litres (2 pints), adding water if needed. Set aside. Strip the meat from the bones, discard the bones, and set the meat aside.

2 Heat the oil in a large, heavy pan. Add the onion and bay leaves, and cook over a medium-low heat for 5–7 minutes until soft. Add the carrots and fennel and cook for 8 more minutes until soft. Stir in the garlic and season with pepper, add the tomatoes, and cook on a low heat for 10 minutes. Ladle in a little stock if it starts to get dry. Add the thyme leaves, nutmeg, chickpeas, beans, and peas, and stir. Add enough stock to cover and simmer gently for 10 minutes. Add the pasta shapes, the reserved meat, and remaining stock. Bring to the boil, then simmer until the pasta is cooked. Add the spinach and stir. Taste and season again, if needed.

STATISTICS PER SERVING

Energy   215kcals/910kJ

Protein   11g

Fat   4g
Saturated fat   0.5g

Carbohydrate   34g
Sugar   7g

Fibre   9.5g

Salt   0.8g

NUTRiENT BOOST
Beetroot is rich in antioxidants and folate.

BEETROOT AND GINGER SOUP

SERVES 4   **PREP** 10 MINS   **COOK** 55 MINS

Earthy beetroot always makes a colourful soup. Here, ginger adds a pleasant zing and the wasabi cream, swirled in at the last minute, gives a fiery kick.

500g (1lb 2oz) raw beetroot, stalks removed
salt
pinch of sugar
1 tbsp olive oil
bunch of spring onions, trimmed and finely chopped
5cm (2in) piece of fresh root ginger, peeled and grated

salt and freshly ground black pepper
750ml (1¼ pints) hot gluten-free vegetable stock
3 tbsp soured cream
¼ tsp wasabi paste, or more if you like it hot

SPECIAL EQUIPMENT food processor or stick blender

1 To cook the beetroot, place them in a pan of salted water, add the sugar, and bring to the boil. Cook on a low-medium heat with the lid ajar for 40 minutes or until the beetroot is tender when poked with a sharp knife. Drain and, when cool enough to handle, peel and roughly chop the beetroot.

2 In a clean pan, heat the oil and add the spring onions. Cook for 2–3 minutes on a medium heat, just enough for them to soften, then add the ginger and cook for a further minute. Add the chopped beetroot and stir well to coat with the oil. Season, pour in the stock, and bring to the boil.

3 Reduce to a simmer and cook gently for about 10 minutes, then ladle into a food processor and blend until smooth, or use a stick blender. Taste and season some more, if needed. Mix the soured cream with the wasabi. Ladle the soup into bowls with a swirl of the wasabi cream.

COOK'S TIP
If you don't have wasabi paste, use gluten-free hot horseradish sauce instead.

STATISTICS PER SERVING

Energy 113kcals/475kJ

Protein 4g

Fat 5.5g

Saturated fat 2g

Carbohydrate 12g

Sugar 12g

Fibre 4g

Salt 0.7g

● ● ● CALORIES

● ● ● SATURATED FAT

● ● ● SALT

SMOKED HADDOCK CHOWDER

SERVES 4   **PREP** 20 MINS   **COOK** 30 MINS

This hearty, creamy soup with delicate white fish and meaty prawns is a meal in itself.

25g (scant 1oz) butter
1 onion, finely chopped
salt and freshly ground black pepper
200g (7oz) smoked pancetta, chopped, or smoked bacon bits
1 bay leaf
3 medium waxy potatoes, such as Charlotte or Maris Peer, peeled and cut into bite-sized pieces
2 tbsp rice flour

1 large glass of dry white wine
300ml (10fl oz) single cream
600ml (1 pint) hot gluten-free fish or vegetable stock
400g can sweetcorn, drained and rinsed
350g (12oz) smoked, undyed haddock, skinned and roughly chopped
250g (9oz) raw, shelled prawns

1 Heat the butter in a large pan, add the onion, and season. Cook on a low heat for 2–3 minutes until softened, then increase the heat a little, add the pancetta and bay leaf, and cook for 4–5 minutes.

2 Turn the heat down, add the potatoes, and stir well to coat with the juices. Tip in the flour and mix thoroughly. Add the wine, increase the heat, and let the wine bubble for 1–2 minutes, stirring occasionally. Stir in the cream and stock, and bring to the boil.

3 Reduce the heat, add the sweetcorn, and simmer gently for about 15 minutes or until the potatoes are cooked. Add the haddock and prawns, cover with a lid, and cook for 4–6 minutes until the fish is just turning opaque and the prawns are pink. Taste and season if necessary.

COOK'S TIP
The secret to a good chowder lies in not overcooking the fish. It will be ready in minutes and will continue cooking in the hot stock once taken off the hob.

STATISTICS PER SERVING

Energy 693kcals/2908kJ

Protein 44g

Fat 33.5g
Saturated fat 17g

Carbohydrate 43g
Sugar 10g

Fibre 3.5g

Salt 3g

ASIAN CRAB AND NOODLE SOUP

SERVES 4   **PREP** 15 MINS   **COOK** 30 MINS
PLUS CHILLING

Prepare this soup a day in advance to allow the flavours to develop, then add the noodles and crab before serving.

1 tbsp sunflower oil
1 bunch of spring onions,
  sliced at an angle
1–2 red chillies, deseeded and
  finely chopped
1–2 garlic cloves, finely chopped
3 carrots, sliced at an angle
326g can sweetcorn, drained
salt and freshly ground black pepper

2 tbsp tamari (gluten-free soy sauce)
750ml (1¼ pints) hot gluten-free
  vegetable stock
100g (3½oz) dried fine rice noodles
400g (14oz) white crab meat
small bunch of chives, finely chopped
small bunch of fresh coriander,
  roughly chopped (see Cook's tip)

1 Heat the oil in a large pan and swirl it around. Add the spring onions and cook over a medium heat for 1 minute until softened. Add the chilli, garlic, carrots, and sweetcorn. Stir and season with salt and pepper.

2 Add the tamari and stir it around so everything gets coated, then add a little of the stock and bring to the boil. Add the rest of the stock, bring to the boil again, partially cover with a lid, reduce to a simmer, and gently cook over a low heat for 15–20 minutes or until the carrots are soft. Set aside to cool, then chill overnight in the fridge to allow the flavours to develop.

3 Place the noodles in a large bowl and pour over enough boiling water to cover. Leave to soak according to pack instructions, then drain.

4 Gently warm the soup, add the noodles, and stir through the crab meat and half the herbs until piping hot. Ladle the soup into bowls and sprinkle with the remaining herbs to serve.

COOK'S TIP
As well as the leaves, use the coriander stalks, which are full of flavour and give a much more distinctive taste than the leaves alone.

STATISTICS PER SERVING

Energy   369kcals/1550kJ

Protein   24g

Fat   9.5g

Saturated fat   1g

Carbohydrate   44g

Sugar   13g

Fibre   4g

Salt   3g

CHINESE CHICKEN SOUP WITH PRAWN DUMPLINGS

GUIDELINES PER SERVING

● ○ ○ CALORIES

● ○ ○ SATURATED FAT

● ● ● SALT

SERVES 4   **PREP** 20 MINS   **COOK** 50 MINS

If you don't have time to make dumplings, simply chop the prawns and stir them straight into the soup.

2 large chicken breasts, skinless
salt and freshly ground black pepper
5 spring onions, sliced at an angle
5cm (2in) piece of fresh root ginger,
  peeled and sliced into matchsticks
1–2 tbsp tamari (gluten-free soy sauce)
½–1 red chilli, thinly sliced at an angle
150g (5½oz) shiitake mushrooms, sliced
125g (4½oz) cooked rice

For the dumplings
350g (12oz) prawns, cooked and peeled
5cm (2in) piece of fresh root ginger,
  peeled and roughly chopped
1 red chilli, deseeded, finely chopped
small handful of coriander leaves,
  plus extra to garnish
2 tsp gluten-free nam pla (fish sauce)
2 tbsp cornflour, plus extra for rolling

1 For the stock, pour 1.5 litres (2¾ pints) water into a large pan and add the chicken breasts and seasoning. Bring to a steady simmer and cook on a low-medium heat, partially covered, for 15–20 minutes until the chicken is cooked. Remove with a slotted spoon and set aside to cool. Strain the stock into a clean pan; you will need about 1.2 litres (2 pints). Shred the chicken and set aside.

2 For the dumplings, place all the ingredients in a food processor, season, and pulse until minced. Scoop up small handfuls and roll into balls; you may need more cornflour. Place the dumplings on a plate and chill in the fridge.

3 Heat the stock over a low-medium heat, add the spring onions, ginger, tamari, chilli, and the mushrooms, and cook for about 20 minutes. Taste and adjust the seasoning as needed.

4 Stir in the rice and shredded chicken and simmer gently for 2 minutes. Add the dumplings, cover, and cook for about 5–8 minutes. Ladle into bowls and top with coriander leaves to serve.

STATISTICS PER SERVING

Energy 250kcals/1047kJ

Protein 36g

Fat 2g
Saturated fat 0.5g

Carbohydrate 19g
Sugar 1g

Fibre 0.9g

Salt 2.5g

QUINOA SALAD WITH MANGO, LIME, AND TOASTED COCONUT

SERVES 4   **PREP** 15 MINS   **COOK** 10 MINS

A healthy salad full of big, tropical flavours and bright colours. Try to get Alphonso mangoes, if possible, which are famed for their sweetness.

50g (1¾oz) desiccated or
  flaked coconut
300g (10oz) quinoa
400g can butter beans, drained
  and rinsed
½ red onion, finely chopped
1 large mango, peeled, stoned, and cut
  into bite-sized pieces
1 lime, peeled, segmented, and
  segments halved

handful of mint, finely chopped
handful of flat-leaf parsley,
  finely chopped

For the dressing
3 tbsp olive oil
1 tbsp white wine vinegar
pinch of sugar
salt and freshly ground black pepper

NUTRiENT BOOST
Mango is an excellent source of betacarotene.

1 Toast the coconut by dry frying it in a pan over a medium heat for 2–3 minutes until golden, stirring so that it doesn't burn. Remove from the heat and allow to cool.

2 To make the dressing, place all the ingredients in a small bowl or jug and whisk. Taste and adjust the seasoning as needed.

3 Cook the quinoa according to pack instructions. Drain well and tip into a large serving bowl. While the quinoa is still warm, stir through the butter beans, onion, mango, lime, mint, and parsley, and season.

4 Pour over the dressing and stir well. Sprinkle the toasted coconut on top and serve immediately.

STATISTICS PER SERVING

Energy 460kcals/1935kJ

Protein 15g

Fat 20g
Saturated fat 8g

Carbohydrate 54g
Sugar 12.5g

Fibre 7.5g

Salt 0.8g

○○○ CALORIES

○○○ SATURATED FAT

○○○ SALT

CHICKPEA, RED RICE, AND ARTICHOKE SALAD

SERVES 4   **PREP** 10 MINS   **COOK** 35 MINS

A substantial main meal salad, it's also good as a side dish to accompany grilled or barbecued salmon or chicken.

400g (14oz) Camargue red rice
400g can chickpeas, drained
  and rinsed
280g jar roasted artichokes, drained
1 red chilli, deseeded and
  finely chopped
handful of fresh coriander,
  finely chopped
handful of flat-leaf parsley,
  finely chopped
2 tbsp pine nuts, toasted
75g (2½oz) feta cheese, crumbled

**For the coriander and
orange dressing**
6 tbsp extra virgin olive oil
2 tbsp white wine vinegar
juice of 1 large orange
1½ tsp coriander seeds,
  lightly crushed
1 tsp Dijon mustard
pinch of sugar
salt and freshly ground black pepper

NUTRIENT BOOST
Soluble fibre in chickpeas helps balance blood sugar and reduce cholesterol.

1 For the dressing, place all the ingredients in a small bowl or jug and mix well. Taste and adjust the seasoning as required.

2 Place the rice in a large pan of salted water and cook according to pack instructions until tender. Drain well and transfer to a serving bowl.

3 While the rice is still warm, stir through the chickpeas, artichokes, chilli, and herbs, and mix well. Pour the dressing over the rice mixture and toss together. Taste and adjust the seasoning. Top with the pine nuts and feta cheese and serve.

STATISTICS PER SERVING

Energy 710kcals/2958kJ

Protein 17g

Fat 28g
Saturated fat 5.5g

Carbohydrate 90g
Sugar 7g

Fibre 5g

Salt 1.3g

COOK'S TIP
Camargue red rice has a slightly nutty taste. You can also use half Camargue rice and half basmati rice.

TUNA AND VEGETABLE PASTA SALAD

SERVES 4   **PREP** 15 MINS   **COOK** 10–15 MINS

Tuna and green beans mix well with pasta in this simple salad. The addition of artichokes makes it extra special.

150g (5½oz) green beans
salt and freshly ground black pepper
250g (9oz) gluten-free pasta shapes
 (shop-bought or see pages 18–19)
150g (5½oz) cherry tomatoes, halved
8 artichoke halves in oil, drained
 and halved

75g (2½oz) pitted green olives, sliced
juice of ½ lemon
2 x 120g cans tuna in oil, drained
 and roughly flaked
extra virgin olive oil, for drizzling
gluten-free bread, to serve

1 Place the beans in a pan of boiling salted water and cook for about 5 minutes until tender. Drain, refresh in cold water, and drain again. Cut each bean into 3 pieces and set aside.

2 Cook the pasta in a large pan of boiling salted water according to instructions. Drain and return to the pan with a little of the cooking water.

3 Place the pasta and beans in a serving bowl, add the tomatoes, artichokes, olives, and lemon juice, and toss together. Add the tuna, drizzle with olive oil, and season to taste with salt and pepper. Serve with some gluten-free bread.

COOK'S TIP
Refreshing the beans in cold water just after cooking helps retain their vibrant colour and keeps them crisp by halting the cooking process.

GUIDELINES PER SERVING

●●○ CALORIES
●○○ SATURATED FAT
●●○ SALT

STATISTICS PER SERVING

Energy 420kcals/1768kJ

Protein 23g

Fat 15g
Saturated fat 2g

Carbohydrate 46g
Sugar 4g

Fibre 5g

Salt 1.2g

PANZANELLA

SERVES 4   **PREP** 10 MINS

This classic Italian salad combines torn bread tossed with
fresh tomatoes and basil.

8 slices of gluten-free white bread,
  crusts removed
handful of basil leaves, torn
extra virgin olive oil, for drizzling
1–2 tbsp balsamic vinegar

sea salt and freshly ground
  black pepper
5 tomatoes, skinned and roughly
  chopped (see Cook's tip)
handful of pitted black olives

1 Tear the bread into chunky pieces and sit them in a bowl. Cover with
a little cold water and leave to soak for 2 minutes. Remove and squeeze
away any excess water, then place in a serving bowl.

2 Add the basil leaves and a drizzle of olive oil. Sprinkle balsamic vinegar
to taste, and season well.

3 When ready to serve, add the tomatoes and olives, and toss together well.
Season to taste and drizzle over more oil if required.

COOK'S TIP
Use firm tomatoes for this salad. It's best made in the summer when full-flavoured
tomatoes are plentiful.

Golden Queen tomatoes »
To add extra visual appeal,
look out for colourful varieties
of tomatoes, such as Golden
Queen. Yellow tomatoes tend
to have a milder flavour,
however, so mix with the
stronger-tasting red varieties.

GUIDELINES PER SERVING

◑○○ CALORIES

◑○○ SATURATED FAT

◑◑○ SALT

GREAT FOR KIDS

STATISTICS PER SERVING

Energy 225kcals/953kJ

Protein 7g

Fat 6g
Saturated fat 1g

Carbohydrate 37g
Sugar 6g

Fibre 3.5g

Salt 1g

⬤⬤◯ CALORIES

⬤⬤⬤ SATURATED FAT

⬤◯◯ SALT

RICOTTA AND SQUASH RAVIOLI

SERVES 4   **PREP** 30 MINS   **COOK** 50-55 MINS   **FREEZE** 1 MONTH
PLUS CHILLING

Make the ravioli a day in advance. Dust them with polenta, place them on a tray covered with cling film, and chill.

175g (6oz) butternut squash, peeled, deseeded, and cut into 5cm (2in) cubes
1 tbsp olive oil
salt and freshly ground black pepper
85g (3oz) ricotta cheese
30g (1oz) Parmesan cheese, finely grated
1 garlic clove, crushed
½ tsp freshly grated nutmeg
350g (12oz) gluten-free pasta dough (see pages 18-19)

gluten-free plain flour, for dusting
polenta or fine cornmeal, for dusting

For the sage butter
3 tbsp olive oil
60g (2oz) butter
zest of ½ lemon
2 tsp roughly chopped sage leaves
finely grated Parmesan cheese, to serve

SPECIAL EQUIPMENT 6cm (2½in) round metal cutter

1 For the filling, preheat the oven to 200°C (400°F/Gas 6). Place the butternut cubes in a roasting tin and drizzle over the oil, 3 tablespoons water, and seasoning. Cover with foil and roast for 30–35 minutes or until tender. Transfer to a food processor and blitz until smooth. Spread in the roasting tin and leave until cold. Place the ricotta, Parmesan cheese, garlic, and nutmeg in a bowl. Stir in the butternut squash and season to taste. Chill.

2 Roll out the pasta dough onto a lightly floured surface to 3mm (⅛in) thick. Cut out 64 rounds using a cutter. Top half the rounds with ½ teaspoon filling. Brush a little water around the filling and place a plain pasta round on top. Pinch the edges to seal. This will make 32 ravioli. Dust with polenta to prevent them from sticking together. Cover and chill until required.

3 Bring a large pan of salted water to the boil. Add the pasta and cook for 4–5 minutes or until al dente. For the sage butter, heat a large frying pan, add the olive oil, butter, lemon zest, and sage, and sauté for 30 seconds. Remove and add plenty of pepper. Drain the pasta in a colander, add to the frying pan, and toss well to mix. Serve sprinkled with Parmesan.

STATISTICS PER SERVING

Energy 640kcals/2670kJ

Protein 16g

Fat 40g
Saturated fat 15g

Carbohydrates 53g
Sugar 3g

Fibre 3g

Salt 1.2g

GREAT FOR KiDS

STATISTICS PER SERVING

Energy 409kcals/1715kJ

Protein 28g

Fat 14.5g

Saturated fat 3g

Carbohydrate 40g

Sugar 4g

Fibre 3g

Salt 0.5g

POLENTA FISHCAKES

SERVES 4   **PREP** 20 MINS   **COOK** 50 MINS   **FREEZE** 1 MONTH
PLUS CHILLING

Polenta makes a crunchy, gluten-free alternative to breadcrumbs for coating fishcakes.

400g (14oz) floury potatoes
400g (14oz) white fish, skin on
200ml (7fl oz) milk
1 bay leaf
knob of butter
1 onion, finely chopped
salt and freshly ground black pepper
handful of flat-leaf parsley,
    finely chopped
2 tsp capers, rinsed and chopped

2 gherkins, roughly chopped
100g (3½oz) polenta or fine cornmeal,
    to coat
leaves from a few sprigs of thyme,
    finely chopped
2 tbsp gluten-free plain flour
1 egg, lightly beaten
3–4 tbsp sunflower oil, for frying
gluten-free tartare sauce and green
    beans, to serve

1 In a large pan, cook the potatoes, still in their skins, in boiling water for 20–30 minutes until soft. Drain and cool, then remove the skins and mash well. Set aside. Sit the fish in a frying pan, add the milk and the bay leaf, then cover and simmer on a gentle heat for 5 minutes until the fish begins to flake. Remove from the heat and discard the bay leaf and most of the milk; keep some back for the potato mix. Discard the skin and bones. When cool enough to handle, pull apart into chunky flakes and set aside.

2 Melt the butter in a frying pan, add the onion, season, and cook on a low heat for 5 minutes until soft. Leave to cool. In a large bowl, add the fish, potatoes, onions, parsley, capers, and gherkins, and stir gently until combined; if the mixture is stiff, add 1–2 tablespoons of the cooking milk to help bind it. Season, divide the mixture into 8 balls, and flatten into cakes.

3 Take 3 plates. Mix the polenta and the thyme and add to 1 plate, the flour to another, and the egg to a third. Dip the cakes into the flour for a light dusting, then dip in the egg, and coat in the polenta. Put on a baking tray and chill in the fridge for 20 minutes; if freezing, do so at this point. To cook, heat a little oil in a non-stick frying pan, add the cakes a few at a time, and cook on a medium heat for 3–4 minutes on each side until golden all over. Top up with oil as needed. Serve with tartare sauce and green beans.

QUICHE LORRAINE

SERVES 6   **PREP** 20 MINS   **COOK** 1 HOUR

A timeless classic that never fails to please. You can add fresh chopped tomatoes into the mix, but do keep this tart simple.

400g (14oz) gluten-free shortcrust
   pastry (see pages 20-21)
gluten-free plain flour, for dusting

For the filling
1 tbsp olive oil
1 onion, finely chopped
salt and freshly ground black pepper
200g (7oz) bacon or pancetta, cubed

200g (7oz) Cheddar cheese, grated
250ml (9fl oz) double cream
3 eggs, lightly beaten
50g (1¾oz) Gruyère cheese, grated

SPECIAL EQUIPMENT 20.5cm (8in)
   round, loose-bottomed tart tin,
   at least 4.5cm (1¾in) deep

1 Preheat the oven to 200°C (400°F/Gas 6). Roll out the pastry on a lightly floured surface to a thickness of 5mm (¼in). Line the tin with the pastry, patching up any holes, then neaten and trim the edges. Prick the base with a fork, line with baking parchment and fill with baking beans, then bake in the oven for 15 minutes. Remove the beans and paper and return to the oven for another 5 minutes to crisp up. Set aside. Reduce the oven temperature to 180°C (350°F/Gas 4).

2 Meanwhile, heat the oil in a frying pan, add the onion, and cook for 6–8 minutes or until beginning to soften. Season to taste with salt and pepper, then transfer to a bowl and set aside to cool. Add the bacon or pancetta to the pan and cook on a medium heat for 5–8 minutes until golden. Set aside.

3 Sprinkle the onion over the base of the pastry case. Add the bacon or pancetta, draining off any excess fat, then add the Cheddar, mixing it up a little. Mix the cream and eggs together and season. Pour the mixture into the case and sprinkle over the Gruyère cheese. Cook for 25–30 minutes until the top is dark golden and the quiche is set. Leave to cool slightly in the tin to set more, then serve warm.

STATISTICS PER SLICE

Energy 838kcals/3478kJ

Protein 25g

Fat 68g
Saturated fat 32g

Carbohydrate 31g
Sugar 2g

Fibre 2g

Salt 2.6g

- ●●○ CALORIES
- ●●● SATURATED FAT
- ●○○ SALT

GREAT FOR KIDS

GOAT'S CHEESE TARTLETS

MAKES 6   **PREP** 30 MINS   **COOK** 25–35 MINS
PLUS CHILLING

Sweet prunes pair well with goat's cheese and the tartlets can be served with sun-dried tomato bread.

100g (3½oz) butter, cubed, plus extra
  for greasing
225g (8oz) gluten-free plain flour, plus
  extra for dusting
pinch of salt
1 tsp xanthan gum
1 tbsp olive oil
1 large red onion, finely sliced
leaves from a few sprigs of thyme

225g (8oz) semi-hard, mild goat's
  cheese, finely cubed
125g (4½oz) pitted soft
  prunes, chopped
freshly ground black pepper

SPECIAL EQUIPMENT 6 x 9cm (3½in)
  round, 2.5cm (1in) deep, tart tins

1 Preheat the oven to 200°C (400°F/Gas 6). Grease the tins with butter. Mix the flour, salt, and xanthan in a bowl. Rub the butter in with your fingertips until it forms crumbs. Gradually add 1–2 tablespoons cold water until the mixture binds to form a dough. Briefly knead the dough on a lightly floured surface until smooth, wrap in cling film, and chill for 10 minutes.

2 Cut the pastry dough into 6 even pieces. Roll out each piece between 2 pieces of cling film and cut 6 x 12cm (5in) rounds. Lift the pastry into the tart tins, pushing it into the base and sides. If it tears, patch it up. Trim the top, prick the bases with a fork, and line each with baking parchment and fill with baking beans. Bake for 10–15 minutes or until the edges turn pale golden. Remove the beans and paper, and set the cases aside.

3 For the filling, heat the oil in a small pan, add the onion and thyme, and cook on a medium heat for 5 minutes until the onion begins to soften and turn transparent. Reduce the heat and cook for a further 5 minutes, to sweeten them a little, then spoon them into the pastry cases.

4 Mix the goat's cheese and prunes and season with pepper. Divide between the cases and bake for 15–20 minutes or until the mixture is bubbling and the pastry is golden brown. Remove and serve warm.

STATISTICS PER TARTLET

Energy 435kcals/1818kJ

Protein 12g

Fat 26g

Saturated fat 16g

Carbohydrate 36g

Sugar 10g

Fibre 4g

Salt 1g

GREAT FOR KIDS

MUSHROOM BURGERS

SERVES 4 **PREP** 20 MINS **COOK** 50 MINS
PLUS CHILLING

Served with miso-roasted chips and tahini dip, these burgers have lots of gutsy flavours. Make mini ones for the kids.

3 tbsp olive oil
1 onion, finely chopped
500g (1lb 2oz) chestnut mushrooms,
  pulsed in a food processor
4 anchovies, finely chopped
tamari (gluten-free soy sauce)
125g (4½oz) gluten-free breadcrumbs
1 egg, lightly beaten
salt and freshly ground black pepper

For the miso chips
4 sweet potatoes, peeled and cut
  into thin chips

1 tbsp olive oil
1 tbsp sweet miso or tamari
  (gluten-free soy sauce)

For the tahini dip
2 garlic cloves, grated
pinch of sea salt
3 tbsp tahini
juice of 1 lemon

SPECIAL EQUIPMENT food processor

1 Preheat the oven to 200°C (400°F/Gas 6). Heat 1 tablespoon oil in a large frying pan, add the onion, and cook on a low heat for 3–4 minutes. Add the mushrooms and cook for 6 minutes or until they start to release their juices. Stir through the anchovies and tamari and cook for 1 minute. Transfer to a large bowl. Add the breadcrumbs and trickle in the egg until the mixture binds well. Add more crumbs if it's too wet and season well. Make 4 large balls from the mixture and form into burgers. Sit them on a baking sheet lined with baking parchment and chill in the fridge for 30 minutes.

2 For the chips, toss the potatoes with the oil and miso or tamari, and spread out in a roasting tin. Roast in the oven for 20 minutes until the chips begin to turn golden and the thinner ones are crisp. For the tahini dip, grind the garlic and sea salt in a pestle and mortar. Add the tahini and mix. Add about 2 tablespoons water to loosen it. Stir through the lemon juice.

3 To cook the burgers, heat half the remaining oil in a large frying pan on a medium heat, add the burgers 2 at a time, and cook for 3–5 minutes on each side, until golden. Repeat to cook the remaining burgers. Serve with the sweet potato chips and tahini dip.

STATISTICS PER SERVING

Energy 509kcals/2143kJ

Protein 13.6g

Fat 21.4g
Saturated fat 3.3g

Carbohydrate 65.3g
Sugar 14g

Fibre 10.8g

Salt 2.8g

BEAN PATTIES

SERVES 4   **PREP** 20 MINS   **COOK** 50 MINS
PLUS CHILLING

Mashed bean patties are a great vegetarian alternative to burgers. If making for kids, omit the chilli and replace half the onion with grated carrot for additional sweetness.

1 onion, quartered
2 tbsp chopped flat-leaf parsley
400g can butter beans, drained
  and rinsed
400g can borlotti beans, drained
  and rinsed
1 tsp cayenne pepper
2 tbsp gluten-free plain flour
1 egg, lightly beaten
salt and freshly ground black pepper
3 tbsp olive oil
green salad, to serve

For the avocado salsa
2 ripe avocados, stoned and diced
1 large garlic clove, grated
1 red chilli, deseeded and
  finely chopped
2 tbsp olive oil
1 tbsp finely chopped fresh coriander
  leaves
juice of 1 lime
1 tsp sugar

SPECIAL EQUIPMENT food processor

1 Place the onion in a food processor and pulse until roughly chopped. Add the parsley and pulse again a couple of times. Then add the beans and pulse again. Transfer to a large bowl and stir in the cayenne pepper, flour, and egg. Season to taste and mix well. Shape the mixture into 8 patties and chill in the fridge until firm.

2 For the salsa, place all the ingredients in a bowl and combine well. Leave for 15 minutes, then stir and season to taste, as needed.

3 Heat a little oil in a large frying pan on a medium-high heat. Add the patties a few at a time and cook for 5 minutes on each side until crisp and golden. Repeat until all are cooked, adding more oil as needed. Serve with a green salad and the salsa on the side.

VARIATION
Other beans, such as cannellini, flageolet, or red kidney beans will work just as well.

NUTRIENT BOOST
Avocados contain vitamins E and B6 for a healthy heart and nervous system.

STATISTICS PER SERVING

Energy 424kcals/1761kJ

Protein 11.5g

Fat 31g
Saturated fat 5.6g

Carbohydrate 25g
Sugar 4g

Fibre 11.5g

Salt 1.4g

SPICED NOODLES WITH AROMATIC RED SNAPPER

SERVES 4 **PREP** 15 MINS **COOK** 25-30 MINS
PLUS MARINATING

Sambal oelek, an Indonesian hot chilli condiment, is the perfect partner for this delicate fish.

1 red snapper, filleted, skinned, and
   chopped into large chunks
250g (9oz) dried fine rice noodles
1 tbsp sunflower oil
bunch of spring onions, sliced
300g (10oz) French beans, trimmed
   and chopped
1 red pepper, deseeded and
   finely chopped
2 garlic cloves, finely chopped
1-2 tsp sambal oelek, or 1 chopped
   red chilli, or ½-1 tsp dried chilli
   flakes mixed with 1 tsp vegetable oil
1 tbsp tamari (gluten-free soy sauce)

handful of fresh coriander, leaves only
1 orange, peeled and segmented

For the marinade
zest and juice of 1 orange
2 tsp finely chopped thyme leaves
1 red chilli, deseeded and finely
   chopped
2 garlic cloves, finely chopped
1 tbsp olive oil
salt and freshly ground black pepper

SPECIAL EQUIPMENT wok or large,
   deep, non-stick frying pan

1 Place the fish in a shallow dish. Combine all the marinade ingredients in a jug, stir well, and pour over the fish, turning the pieces to coat. Set aside to marinate for up to 1 hour. Preheat the oven to 180°C (350°F/Gas 4). Remove the fish using a slotted spoon and place in a roasting tin. Roast for 20–25 minutes or until the fish is cooked through and turning opaque. Set aside.

2 Cover the noodles with boiling water and leave for 10 minutes or as per pack instructions. Drain. Add the oil to the wok or pan and swirl it around. Add the spring onions and cook on a medium-high heat for 2–3 minutes until soft. Add the beans and stir. Cook for about 5 minutes until they begin to soften. Stir in the pepper and garlic and cook for 2–3 minutes.

3 Add the sambal oelek and tamari. Add the noodles and toss. Cook for 3–5 minutes and transfer to a serving dish. Top with the fish and coriander. Serve with the orange segments.

STATISTICS PER SERVING

Energy 473kcals/1982kJ

Protein 35g

Fat 8g
Saturated fat 1g

Carbohydrate 59g
Sugar 11g

Fibre 4g

Salt 1g

○○○ CALORIES

○○○ SATURATED FAT

○○○ SALT

ASIAN-STYLE CRISPY FISH

SERVES 4   **PREP** 20 MINS   **COOK** 15 MINS

A medley of vegetables topped with pan-fried red mullet and seasoned with a Vietnamese-style dressing.

4 red mullet, gurnard or sea bass
  fillets, skinned
1 tbsp rice flour
1 tbsp sunflower oil

For the noodles and vegetables
250g (9oz) vermicelli rice noodles
200g (7oz) pak choi, trimmed
  and shredded
2 carrots, grated
handful of beansprouts
4 spring onions, finely sliced
handful of mint leaves, torn

handful of Thai basil leaves or
  regular basil, torn
handful of fresh coriander leaves
1 tbsp sesame seeds, to garnish

For the dressing
juice of 2 limes
2 tbsp rice wine vinegar
gluten-free nam pla (fish sauce)

SPECIAL EQUIPMENT wok or large, deep
  non-stick frying pan

1 For the dressing, mix together the lime juice and rice wine vinegar. Add the nam pla to taste, and set aside.

2 Toss the fish fillets in the rice flour, heat the oil in the wok or pan, and add them to the hot oil. Cook 2 at a time on a medium-high heat for about 4–6 minutes turning halfway until golden and crispy. Remove with a fish slice and set aside on a plate layered with kitchen paper, to drain. Repeat to cook the remaining fillets.

3 Sit the noodles in a bowl, pour over boiling water to cover, and leave for 3–4 minutes, or as per pack instructions. Drain well, separate the strands if needed, and set aside to cool. In a large bowl, place the shredded pak choi, grated carrot, and half the dressing and toss. Add the beansprouts, spring onions, and cooled noodles and toss again with the remaining dressing. Add half the herbs, toss, and transfer to a serving dish. Top with the fish fillets and sprinkle over the remaining herbs and sesame seeds.

STATISTICS PER SERVING

Energy 488kcals/2043kJ

Protein 34g

Fat 11g

Saturated fat 1g

Carbohydrate 56g

Sugar 5g

Fibre 4g

Salt 0.6g

BEER-BATTERED FISH AND CHIPS

SERVES 4   **PREP** 15 MINS   **COOK** 40 MINS

A favourite classic – the batter serves as a protective casing while the fish cooks, leaving it flaky and delicate.

800g (1¾lb) potatoes, peeled and
  cut into thickish fingers
3 tbsp olive oil
pinch of sea salt
4 haddock or cod fillets, skin on
salt and freshly ground black pepper
juice of ½ lemon
225g (8oz) gluten-free self-raising
  flour, sifted, plus extra for dusting

300ml (10fl oz) gluten-free beer
vegetable oil, for frying
lemon wedges and gluten-free tartare
  sauce and green beans, to serve

SPECIAL EQUIPMENT deep-fat
  fryer (optional)

1 For the chips, preheat the oven to 200°C (400°F/Gas 6). Tip the potatoes into a large roasting tin, add the olive oil, and coat them well. Spread them out so they roast rather than steam, and sprinkle with sea salt. Cook in the oven for 30–40 minutes until golden, turning them halfway through cooking.

2 Meanwhile, season the fish, squeeze a little lemon juice over each fillet, and dust with a little flour. Place the remaining flour along with a pinch of salt to a bowl and slowly pour in the beer, whisking as you go. You may not need all the beer, as the mixture should be thick. If it is too runny, it won't stick to the fish, so stop when you reach the required consistency.

3 Fill a deep-fat fryer with the vegetable oil, or pour it into a large pan so that it is one-third full, and heat to 190°C (375°F); maintain this temperature throughout. Do not leave the pan or fryer unattended, switch off when not using, and keep a fire blanket nearby in case of fire. Hold the fish by the tail and pass it through the batter so that it's completely coated, then add it to the oil. Cook 2 fillets at a time for 2–3 minutes, turn over, and cook for a further 2–3 minutes until crisp and golden. Transfer to kitchen paper to drain and repeat with the remaining fish, keeping the finished pieces warm in a low oven. Serve with the chips, lemon wedges and tartare sauce.

STATISTICS PER SERVING

Energy 703kcals/2955kJ

Protein 37g

Fat 26g
Saturated fat 3.5g

Carbohydrate 73g
Sugar 3.5g

Fibre 5.8g

Salt 1.3g

● ● ○ CALORIES

● ● ● SATURATED FAT

● ● ● SALT

SMOKED SALMON PASTA

SERVES 4   **PREP** 10 MINS   **COOK** 15 MINS

Cream cheese makes an instant and cheap pasta sauce for this easy mid-week supper dish.

350g (12oz) gluten-free linguine or
  other pasta shapes (see pages 18-19)
200g (7oz) cream cheese
250g (9oz) smoked salmon
  trimmings, chopped

2–3 sprigs of dill, finely chopped
salt and freshly ground black pepper
wild rocket leaves dressed with olive
  oil and lemon juice, to serve

1 Put the pasta in a large pan of boiling salted water and cook according to instructions. Give it a stir at the beginning of cooking to prevent it from sticking together. Drain and return to the pan with a little of the cooking water.

2 Stir the cream cheese through the pasta, so it melts to form a sauce. Add the salmon and stir again.

3 Sprinkle over the dill and season. Serve with a lightly dressed, lemony wild rocket salad.

COOK'S TIP
For a more sophisticated version, swap the cream cheese for fresh ricotta.

STATISTICS PER SERVING

Energy 636kcals/2669kJ

Protein 26g

Fat 31g
Saturated fat 16g

Carbohydrate 62g
Sugar 2g

Fibre 3.5g

Salt 2.5g

CRAB AND TOMATO PASTA

SERVES 4   **PREP** 15 MINS   **COOK** 30 MINS

Pasta absorbs wonderfully the sweet flavour of crab.
This is an easy dish for last-minute entertaining.

1 tbsp olive oil
1 onion, very finely chopped
1 celery stick, very finely chopped
1 bay leaf
salt and freshly ground black pepper
2 garlic cloves, finely chopped
1 red chilli, deseeded and
  finely chopped

100ml (3½fl oz) dry white wine
150ml (5fl oz) passata
350g (12oz) gluten-free linguine
  or other pasta shapes (see pages
  18-19)
250g (9oz) fresh white crab meat
handful of flat-leaf parsley,
  finely chopped

1 Heat the oil in a large pan, add the onion, and cook over a low heat for 5–6 minutes until soft. Add the celery, bay leaf, and salt and pepper, and cook gently on a low heat, stirring, for about 10 minutes, making sure the vegetables don't brown. Stir in the garlic and chilli, and cook for another minute.

2 Raise the heat, add the wine, and let it bubble for 1 minute. Add the passata and let this bubble for 2–3 minutes. Reduce to a low heat and simmer gently for about 15 minutes.

3 Put the pasta in a large pan of boiling salted water and cook according to instructions. Give it a stir at the beginning of cooking to prevent it from sticking together. Drain and return to the pan with a little of the cooking water. Stir the crab meat into the tomato sauce and warm through. Pour the sauce over the linguine and toss to combine. Sprinkle over the parsley and serve straight away.

Fresh crab »
If buying whole crab or cooking your own crab, the white meat can be found in the central body, legs, and claws. Use a lobster or nut-cracker to break the shell and extract the flesh with a lobster pick or skewer.

STATISTICS PER SERVING

Energy 446kcals/1888kJ

Protein 23g

Fat 8g
Saturated fat 1g

Carbohydrate 66g
Sugar 3.5g

Fibre 4.5g

Salt 0.7g

● ● ○ CALORIES

● ○ ○ SATURATED FAT

● ○ ○ SALT

HOT SPICED RICE WITH CHICKEN AND POMEGRANATE

SERVES 4   **PREP** 15 MINS   **COOK** 35-40 MINS
PLUS MARINATING

The heady spice mix elevates this easy chicken dish – plus it's a real feast for the eyes!

½ tsp ground cinnamon
½ tsp ground allspice
½ tsp ground cloves
½ tsp ground coriander
salt and freshly ground black pepper
juice of 1 orange
150ml (5fl oz) pomegranate juice
  (see Cook's tip)

2 garlic cloves, finely chopped
8 chicken thighs, skin on
3 courgettes, thickly sliced
300g (10oz) basmati rice
1-2 Scotch bonnet chillies, left whole
150g (5½oz) pomegranate seeds,
  or seeds from 1 pomegranate

1 Preheat the oven to 200°C (400°F/Gas 6). Mix all the spices with the salt and pepper, orange juice, pomegranate juice, and garlic. Place the chicken pieces in a roasting tin and pour over half the mixture to coat. Cover and marinate for 30 minutes, then roast in the oven for 20–25 minutes. Add the courgettes to the roasting tin and cook for another 15 minutes or until the chicken is golden and the skin begins to char slightly.

2 Meanwhile, place the rice and chillies in a pan, and top up with water so it just covers the rice. Season with salt and tip in the remaining spice mix. Cook on a medium heat with the lid ajar for 15 minutes until the rice has absorbed all the water and is just cooked. Turn off the heat, sit the lid on top, and leave for 10 minutes to steam.

3 Transfer the rice to a serving dish, top with the chicken and any juices, and the courgettes, and sprinkle with the pomegranate seeds to serve. Use Scotch bonnets for garnish, or chop and scatter over the dish for some heat.

STATISTICS PER SERVING

Energy 518kcals/2174kJ

Protein 38g

Fat 8g

Saturated fat 2g

Carbohydrate 68g

Sugar 13g

Fibre 2g

Salt 0.35g

COOK'S TIP
Make fresh pomegranate juice by squashing the seeds from 3 fresh pomegranates through a sieve. Alternatively, try pomegranate molasses for a more intense flavour.

CREAMY CHICKEN CRUMBLE

SERVES 4   **PREP** 20 MINS   **COOK** 45 MINS–1 HOUR   **FREEZE** 1 MONTH

If serving this for children, replace the wine with gluten-free stock. You could also stir in sweetcorn kernels and replace the chicken with cooked ham.

2 large chicken breasts, skin on
1 tbsp olive oil
salt and freshly ground black pepper
steamed leeks, to serve

For the crumble topping
150g (5½oz) rice flour
pinch of salt
75g (2½oz) butter, cubed
3 tbsp grated Parmesan cheese
50g (1¾oz) Cheddar cheese, grated
1 tsp mustard seeds, crushed

For the sauce
50g (1¾oz) butter
200g (7oz) baby button mushrooms,
   left whole
1 tbsp rice flour or cornflour
125ml (4fl oz) dry white wine
   or gluten-free chicken stock
150ml (5fl oz) milk
150ml (5fl oz) single cream
1 tbsp Dijon mustard
a few tarragon leaves, chopped

1 Preheat the oven to 200°C (400°F/Gas 6). Place the chicken in a roasting tin, drizzle with the oil, and season. Roast in the oven for 25–35 minutes until golden and cooked through. Don't overcook or it will be dry. Leave to cool slightly, remove the skin, and shred into chunky pieces.

2 For the crumble topping, place the rice flour and salt in a medium bowl. Add the butter and rub it in with your fingers until it resembles breadcrumbs. Stir through the cheeses and mustard seeds. Set aside.

3 For the sauce, melt the butter in a medium pan, add the mushrooms, and cook on a low-medium heat for 5 minutes until golden. Remove the pan, stir in the rice flour, add the wine, and stir again. Return it to the heat and cook for 2–3 minutes, stirring continuously. Add the milk and cream and bring to a gentle boil. Reduce to a simmer, stirring continuously to remove any lumps. As it thickens, stir in the mustard and tarragon leaves, and season.

4 Remove the pan and add the shredded chicken. Stir to coat, spoon into a shallow 1 litre (1¾ pint) ovenproof dish, and top with the crumble mixture. Bake in the oven for 20–25 minutes until golden. Serve with steamed leeks.

STATISTICS PER SERVING

Energy 712kcals/2960kJ

Protein 33g

Fat 45g
Saturated fat 27g

Carbohydrate 34g
Sugar 3g

Fibre 1.5g

Salt 1.6g

CHICKEN AND PARSLEY POT PIES

SERVES 4   **PREP** 20 MINS   **COOK** 25–30 MINS   **FREEZE** 1 MONTH
PLUS CHILLING

These pies are great to make after a roast chicken dinner or to use up leftover ham, and can also be prepared ahead and stored in the fridge overnight before glazing and baking.

150g (5½oz) frozen broad beans,
  or 400g can sweetcorn, drained
50g (1¾oz) butter
1 onion, finely chopped
salt and freshly ground black pepper
50g (1¾oz) gluten-free plain flour,
  plus extra for dusting
450ml (15fl oz) milk
1 tsp Dijon mustard
300g (10oz) cooked chicken, cut
  into chunky bite-sized pieces
150g (5½oz) gluten-free cooked
  ham, cubed

3 tbsp finely chopped curly or
  flat-leaf parsley
1 tbsp finely chopped marjoram
  leaves (optional)
300g (10oz) gluten-free rough puff
  pastry or shortcrust pastry (see
  pages 20-23)
1 egg, beaten
boiled potatoes and carrots, to serve

SPECIAL EQUIPMENT
4 x 300ml (10fl oz) or 1 x 1.2 litre
  (2 pint) pudding basins

1 Preheat the oven to 200°C (400°F/Gas 6). Place the broad beans in a bowl and pour over boiling water. Leave for 5–8 minutes, drain, and set aside.

2 Melt the butter in a large pan over a low heat, add the onion, season, and cook for 5–7 minutes until soft and transparent. Remove from the heat and stir in the flour. Pour in a little milk, stir, put back on a low heat, and gradually add the rest of the milk, stirring as you go. You may need to switch to a balloon whisk for a lump-free sauce. Bring to the boil, then reduce to a simmer. Cook for 2–3 minutes, remove from the heat, and stir in the mustard, chicken, ham, herbs, and broad beans. Season and set aside.

3 Roll out the pastry on a lightly floured surface. Cut out 4 small lids or 1 large lid 4cm (1½in) larger than the basins. Set aside. Spoon the filling into the basins and wet the edges. Drape the lids and press to secure. Make a hole in the top of each pie. Brush with half the beaten egg and chill for 20 minutes, then brush with the remaining egg and bake for 25–30 minutes until golden; cooking a large pie may take a little longer. Remove and serve.

STATISTICS PER SERVING

Energy 703kcals/2942kJ

Protein 43g

Fat 39g

Saturated fat 19g

Carbohydrate 46g

Sugar 9g

Fibre 4g

Salt 2.3g

NUTRIENT BOOST
Peanuts are a good source of vitamin E and fats beneficial to the heart.

CHICKEN AND PEANUT STEW

SERVES 4   **PREP** 30 MINS   **COOK** 45–50 MINS

Full of Caribbean flavours, this spicy stew works well with polenta-coated croquettes and can also be served with rice.

2 tbsp olive oil
500g (1lb 2oz) chicken breast, skinless, cut into bite-sized pieces
salt and freshly ground black pepper
2 onions, finely chopped
2 tsp ground allspice
pinch of freshly grated nutmeg
leaves from a few sprigs of thyme
2 carrots, sliced at an angle
2 red peppers, finely chopped
50g (1¾oz) peanuts (shelled weight) from whole, unshelled peanuts, roughly chopped
2 red chillies, deseeded and finely chopped

3 garlic cloves, finely chopped
1 tbsp tomato purée
300ml (10fl oz) hot gluten-free chicken or vegetable stock
handful of fresh coriander leaves, roughly chopped
plain yogurt, to serve (optional)

For the croquettes
500g (1lb 2oz) floury potatoes, boiled and mashed with salt and pepper and 50g (1¾oz) butter
2 tbsp finely chopped flat-leaf parsley
100g (3½oz) polenta or fine cornmeal

1 Heat half the oil in a heavy pan, season the chicken, and add to the pan. Cook on a medium-high heat for 6–8 minutes or until starting to colour. Remove and set aside. Heat the remaining oil, add the onion, and cook on a low heat for 2–3 minutes. Stir through the allspice, nutmeg, and thyme, add the carrots, and cook for 5 minutes. Add the peppers and cook for 2–3 minutes. Return the chicken to the pan and stir in the peanuts, chilli, and garlic. Cook for 2 minutes, then add the tomato purée and combine well.

2 Add the stock and bring to the boil. Reduce to a simmer, cover, and cook on a low heat for 25–30 minutes, stirring occasionally, until slightly thick. Top up with a little hot water if needed. Season to taste and stir in the coriander.

3 Meanwhile, for the croquettes, preheat the oven to 190°C (375°F/Gas 5). Mix the potato and parsley, divide the mixture into 16 balls and roll each into a sausage. Sprinkle the polenta onto a plate and roll each croquette in it so that they are coated evenly. Place on a lightly greased baking tray and bake in the oven for 25–30 minutes until golden brown and crisp.

STATISTICS PER SERVING

Energy 610kcals/2552kJ

Protein 40g

Fat 25g

Saturated fat 9g

Carbohydrate 51g

Sugar 13g

Fibre 7g

Salt 0.7g

CASSOULET

SERVES 6   **PREP** 15 MINS   **COOK** 2½ HOURS

This intensely rich French stew is well worth the wait and lovely to cook on a cold winter's day.

4 duck legs
3 tbsp olive oil
salt and freshly ground black pepper
1kg (2¼lb) rindless belly pork, cut into bite-sized pieces
6 gluten-free Toulouse sausages, each cut into 4
3 carrots, sliced
2 onions, finely sliced
4 garlic cloves, finely chopped
4 tomatoes, skinned and finely chopped

2 x 400g cans haricot beans, drained and rinsed
1 bouquet garni
300–400ml (10–14fl oz) hot gluten-free chicken stock
handful of gluten-free breadcrumbs
Savoy cabbage or green beans, to serve

SPECIAL EQUIPMENT large flameproof casserole or lidded ovenproof pan

NUTRIENT BOOST
All canned beans are a great source of fibre, protein, and minerals.

1 Preheat the oven to 220°C (425°F/Gas 7). Rub the duck legs with 1 tablespoon oil and then sprinkle and rub all over with salt. Put in a roasting tin and bake in the oven for 15–20 minutes until brown and crisp. Remove and set aside. Reduce the oven temperature to 170°C (340°F/Gas 3½).

2 In the large flameproof casserole, heat the remaining oil on a medium heat, add the pork and cook, stirring frequently, until it begins to brown. Add the sausages and cook for 4–5 minutes, then add the carrots and cook for 5 minutes. Add the onions and cook for 2 minutes. Stir in the garlic, cook for 1 minute, then add the tomatoes, beans, and bouquet garni and season well.

3 Add 300ml (10fl oz) stock to the pan; check as it cooks and add more stock if the cassoulet looks like it's drying out. Cover and cook in the oven for 1 hour, then add the duck legs, combine well, leave uncovered, and cook for a further 1 hour. Sprinkle over the breadcrumbs for the last 30 minutes of cooking; cover loosely with foil if it begins to brown too much. Stir occasionally. When ready, remove the bouquet garni and serve piping hot with Savoy cabbage or green beans.

STATISTICS PER SERVING

Energy 700kcals/2930kJ

Protein 67g

Fat 36g
Saturated fat 11g

Carbohydrate 25g
Sugar 9g

Fibre 6g

Salt 2.9g

● ● ○ CALORIES

● ● ● SATURATED FAT

● ○ ○ SALT

BEEF AND BEER CASSEROLE

SERVES 6   **PREP** 40 MINS   **COOK** 2 HOURS

A really hearty dish with slow-cooked beef simmered in a light beer. Perfect comfort food.

1 tbsp rice flour
salt and freshly ground black pepper
1kg (2¼lb) braising steak, chuck, or
   skirt, cut into large bite-sized pieces
3 tbsp olive oil
300g (10oz) carrots, cut into chunks
1 celeriac, peeled and chopped into
   bite-sized pieces
3 leeks, trimmed, washed, and cut
   into chunks
300ml (10fl oz) gluten-free beer
750ml (1¼ pints) hot gluten-free
   vegetable stock
50g (1¾oz) quinoa

For the herb dumplings
½ onion, finely chopped
½ tbsp olive oil
small handful of flat-leaf parsley,
   finely chopped
a few rosemary leaves, finely chopped
75g (2½oz) gluten-free breadcrumbs
1 tsp gluten-free ready-grated
   horseradish (from a jar)
1 tsp Dijon mustard
1 egg

SPECIAL EQUIPMENT large flameproof
   casserole or lidded ovenproof pan

1 Preheat the oven to 160°C (325°F/Gas 3). Season the flour and toss the beef to coat. Heat 2 tablespoons oil in the casserole and brown the beef in batches over a medium heat for 5 minutes per batch, until sealed. Set aside.

2 Add the remaining oil to the casserole and cook the vegetables for 5–6 minutes, until golden. Pour in a little of the beer, raise the heat, and stir to scrape up any bits from the bottom of the casserole. Add the remaining beer and simmer on a medium heat for 5 minutes. Pour in the stock, bring to the boil, reduce to a simmer, return the meat to the casserole along with the quinoa. Season, cover, and cook in the oven for 1½ hours before adding the dumplings; top up with hot water if it looks dry.

3 For the dumplings, cook the onion in the oil in a medium pan over a medium heat until soft. Add the remaining ingredients, season, and stir until it comes together. Form 12 dumpling balls and set aside. When ready, remove the casserole and add the balls, pushing them down into the sauce. Re-cover and cook for 30 minutes, removing the lid for the last 5 minutes.

Energy 691kcals/2885kJ

Protein 49g

Fat 30g
Saturated fat 12g

Carbohydrate 44g
Sugar 7.5g

Fibre 0.7g

Salt 1.4g

MOUSSAKA

SERVES 4   **PREP** 20 MINS   **COOK** 1 HOUR   **FREEZE** 3 MONTHS

This version of the Greek classic uses beef instead of lamb, but feel free to swap it around. Feta cheese is a tasty addition to the topping instead of Cheddar.

3 tbsp olive oil
2 onions, finely chopped
salt and freshly ground black pepper
400g (14oz) beef mince
4 anchovies, finely chopped
3 garlic cloves, finely chopped
1 tbsp tomato purée
1 tsp dried oregano, plus extra
  for topping
leaves from a few sprigs of thyme

300ml (10fl oz) hot gluten-free
  vegetable stock
2 aubergines, cut into 1cm (½in) slices
200ml (7fl oz) Greek yogurt
1 egg
100g (3½oz) Cheddar cheese, grated
green salad, to serve

SPECIAL EQUIPMENT 22 x 28cm (8¾
  x 11in) ovenproof dish, griddle pan

1 Preheat the oven to 180°C (350°F/Gas 4). In a large, non-stick pan, heat 1 tablespoon oil, add the onions, fry over a low heat for 3–4 minutes, and season. Stir in the beef mince and anchovies and cook for 5 minutes, stirring constantly and breaking up with a fork, until all the meat is sealed and browned. Stir through the garlic and cook for 2 minutes. Add the tomato purée, oregano, and thyme and combine well. Add the stock, increase the heat a little, and bubble for 1–2 minutes. Reduce to a simmer, cover, and cook gently for 15–20 minutes or until the mixture starts to dry out.

2 While the mince is cooking, brush the aubergine slices with the remaining oil and season well. Heat a griddle pan. When hot, add a few slices at a time and cook for 5 minutes on each side or until golden. Remove and sit them on a plate lined with kitchen paper. Repeat until all are cooked.

3 Layer the beef mixture and the aubergine in the ovenproof dish and set aside. Mix together the yogurt and egg in a bowl and whisk with a fork until combined. Pour evenly over the meat mixture, then sprinkle on the cheese and scatter over the oregano. Bake in the oven for 30 minutes or until the top is golden; cover with foil if it starts to brown too much. Serve with a lightly dressed crisp green salad.

STATISTICS PER SERVING

Energy 524kcals/2175kJ

Protein 33g

Fat 38g
Saturated fat 16g

Carbohydrate 8g
Sugar 7g

Fibre 2.5g

Salt 1.4g

GREAT FOR KiDS

NUTRiENT BOOST
Lean red meat is an excellent source of iron.

STATISTICS PER SERVING

Energy 601kcals/2521kJ

Protein 28g

Fat 24g

Saturated fat 7.5g

Carbohydrate 61g

Sugar 8g

Fibre 5g

Salt 0.7g

PASTA AND MEATBALLS

SERVES 4   **PREP** 20 MINS   **COOK** 40 MINS
PLUS CHILLING

Anchovies add richness to the meatballs without giving them a "fishy" flavour. Replace the red wine with 150ml (5fl oz) gluten-free beef stock for a child-friendly version.

1 red onion, finely chopped
300g (10oz) minced beef
pinch of dried chilli flakes
handful of flat-leaf parsley,
   finely chopped
3 anchovy fillets, chopped (optional)
rice flour, for dusting
2–3 tbsp olive oil
300g (10oz) gluten-free spaghetti
   or tagliatelle (see pages 18–19)

For the sauce
1 tbsp olive oil
1 onion, finely chopped
salt and freshly ground black pepper
1 small glass red wine
400g can chopped tomatoes
pinch of dried oregano
freshly grated Parmesan cheese,
   to serve

1 Place the onion, beef, chilli flakes, parsley, and anchovies (if using) in a large bowl, and mix well with your hands, so that the mixture is tightly packed. With floured hands, scoop out golf-ball sized portions and roll until neat. It should make about 12. Sit them on a baking sheet lined with parchment paper and chill in the fridge to firm up.

2 Heat a little oil in a large non-stick frying pan with a lid and add the meatballs a few at a time. Cook on a medium-high heat until browned on all sides, about 6–8 minutes. Repeat with all the meatballs, adding more oil as needed. Transfer to a plate lined with kitchen paper to drain.

3 For the sauce, use the same frying pan to heat the oil, add the onion, season, and cook over a low heat for 3–4 minutes until soft. Tip in the wine, raise the heat, and let it bubble for 2–3 minutes. Reduce to a simmer. Add the tomatoes and oregano and cook gently for 5 minutes. Add the meatballs to the sauce and cook on a low heat with the lid ajar for 20 minutes, turning occasionally and topping up with hot water, if it appears to be drying out. Cook the pasta according to instructions. Season the sauce as needed. Serve with the pasta, topped with grated Parmesan cheese.

GNOCCHI WITH BLUE CHEESE

SERVES 4   **PREP** 30 MINS   **COOK** 50-65 MINS   **FREEZE** 3 MONTHS
UNCOOKED GNOCCHI

A few ingredients make up this delicious dish – delicate gnocchi tossed in sage butter and topped with Gorgonzola.

1kg (2¼lb) starchy potatoes, such as King Edward, Desirée, or Maris Piper, skin on
salt and freshly ground black pepper
150g (5½oz) rice flour, plus extra for dusting

pinch of freshly grated nutmeg
sea salt
50g (1¾oz) butter
4 sage leaves, torn
125g (4½oz) Gorgonzola cheese, cubed
wild rocket and tomato salad, to serve

1 Cook the whole potatoes in a large pan of boiling salted water until tender, about 30–40 minutes. Drain and leave until cool enough to handle. Peel and press the potatoes through a potato ricer onto a lightly floured surface; if you don't have a ricer, use a medium sieve but take care not to over-work the potato. Add half the rice flour, nutmeg, and the sea salt. Lightly knead until the mixture starts to come together, adding more flour as needed. Don't over-knead or the gnocchi will be tough when cooked. Divide the dough into 4. Roll each piece into a sausage shape about 1cm (½in) thick, then slice into 2cm (¾in) pieces, about 80–90 in total.

2 Preheat the oven to 190°C (375°F/Gas 5). Bring a large pan of water to a rolling boil. Add 10 gnocchi at a time, as they need lots of room; they will float to the top once cooked, about 2 minutes. Remove with a slotted spoon, transfer to a warmed ovenproof serving dish, and season with sea salt.

3 Heat the butter in a small frying pan, add the sage leaves, and cook on a medium heat for 2–3 minutes until the butter melts. Pour over the gnocchi and turn to coat. Sprinkle over the cubed cheese, then bake in the oven for 5–6 minutes. Serve with a wild rocket and tomato salad.

COOK'S TIP
To freeze, lay the uncooked gnocchi on a parchment-lined baking sheet and open freeze until solid, then transfer to an airtight freezer container. Cook from frozen, as above, for 3-5 minutes or until the gnocchi float to the surface.

STATISTICS PER SERVING

Energy 532kcals/2222kJ

Protein 14.5g

Fat 22g
Saturated fat 14g

Carbohydrate 65g
Sugar 1.5g

Fibre 5g

Salt 1.1g

GREAT FOR KiDS

PASTA PRIMAVERA

SERVES 4   **PREP** 15 MINS   **COOK** 30 MINS

Serve this light and fresh vegetarian dish in spring, when young, tender vegetables are easily available.

200g (7oz) green beans, trimmed
1 bunch of fine asparagus, trimmed
350g (12oz) gluten-free linguine
   or other pasta shapes (see pages
   18-19)
1 tbsp olive oil

3 courgettes, halved lengthways
   and chopped
salt and freshly ground black pepper
pinch of saffron threads (optional)
4 tomatoes, roughly chopped
grated Parmesan or Pecorino cheese,
   to serve

1 Place the beans in a pan of boiling salted water and cook for 4–5 minutes until tender but still with some bite. Remove with a slotted spoon (reserve the water in the pan), refresh in cold water, and roughly chop. Add the asparagus to the reserved boiling water and cook for 6–8 minutes until almost tender. Drain, refresh, and roughly chop.

2 Put the pasta in a large pan of boiling salted water and cook according to instructions. Give it a stir at the beginning of cooking to prevent it from sticking together. Drain well, return to the pan with a little of the cooking water, and toss together to combine.

3 Meanwhile, heat the oil in a large frying pan, add the courgettes, and season. Add the saffron threads (if using) and cook on a low-medium heat for about 10 minutes until the courgettes turn golden.

4 Add the beans, asparagus, and tomatoes to the frying pan. Stir and cook over a low heat for 5 minutes. Tip the vegetables into the pasta and toss to combine. Serve with the Parmesan or Pecorino and more freshly ground black pepper, if you wish.

COOK'S TIP
Swap the asparagus for frozen peas, if asparagus is not in season.

STATISTICS PER SERVING

Energy   384kcals/1629kJ

Protein   15g

Fat   5g
Saturated fat   1g

Carbohydrate   68g
Sugar   6g

Fibre   8g

Salt   0.1g

PUMPKIN, SPINACH, AND GORGONZOLA LASAGNE

SERVES 4　　**PREP** 25-30 MINS　　**COOK** 1-1¼ HOURS　　**FREEZE** 1 MONTH

This vegetarian lasagne is rich and satisfying, with fresh sage and nutmeg bringing the flavours alive.

about 800g (1¾lb) small pumpkin or
　butternut squash, peeled, deseeded,
　and chopped into bite-sized pieces
1 tbsp olive oil
salt and freshly ground black pepper
8 sage leaves, roughly chopped
pinch of freshly grated nutmeg
pinch of dried chilli flakes (optional)
pinch of allspice
200g (7oz) spinach
10 gluten-free pre-cooked lasagne
　sheets (see pages 18-19)

125g (4½oz) Gorgonzola
　cheese, chopped
lightly dressed green salad, to serve

For the sauce
100g (3½oz) butter
2 tbsp gluten-free plain flour
　or rice flour
900ml (1½ pints) milk

SPECIAL EQUIPMENT 20 x 30cm
　(8 x 12in) ovenproof dish

1 Preheat the oven to 200°C (400°F/Gas 6). Place the pumpkin in a large roasting tin, add the oil and plenty of seasoning, and stir to coat; the tin must be large or the pumpkin will steam rather than roast. Sprinkle over the sage, nutmeg, chilli (if using), and allspice and stir. Roast for 20–30 minutes, stirring halfway, until golden, then remove. Stir in the spinach, which will wilt in a few minutes. Set aside. Reduce the oven temperature to 190°C (375°F/Gas 5).

2 For the sauce, melt the butter in a medium pan. Remove, add the flour, and stir. Add a little milk, stir, and return to the heat. Cook over a low heat, adding the milk and stirring with a wooden spoon. As it thickens, switch to a balloon whisk and stir to remove any lumps. Season well and set aside.

3 For the lasagne, spoon half the pumpkin mixture into the ovenproof dish. Seasoning well between each layer, add half the lasagne sheets, half the sauce, and half the Gorgonzola. Repeat to use up all the ingredients. Place on a baking tray and bake for 30–40 minutes until golden and bubbling. Serve with a lightly dressed green salad.

NUTRIENT BOOST
Spinach is a good source of vitamin K, which is important for healthy bones.

STATISTICS PER SERVING

Energy　531kcals/2221kJ

Protein　19g

Fat　30g
Saturated fat　16g

Carbohydrate　47g
Sugar　10g

Fibre　6g

Salt　1.8g

CALORIES

SATURATED FAT

SALT

Butternut squash is exceptionally rich in vitamin B6.

STATISTICS PER SERVING

Energy 555kcals/2320kJ

Protein 23g

Fat 38g

Saturated fat 14g

Carbohydrate 31g

Sugar 18g

Fibre 11g

Salt 1g

STUFFED BUTTERNUT SQUASH

SERVES 4   **PREP** 15 MINS   **COOK** 1¼ HOURS

A vibrantly coloured autumnal dish that would work just as well with pumpkin. You could use Cheddar, Parmesan, or goat's cheese instead of the Gruyère.

2 medium, or 4 small, butternut
  squash, halved lengthways
  and deseeded
1 tbsp olive oil, plus extra for greasing
225g (8oz) Gruyère cheese, grated

For the fruit and nut mix
100g (3½oz) hazelnuts, toasted and
  roughly chopped

75g (2½oz) dried cranberries,
  roughly chopped
small handful of flat-leaf parsley,
  finely chopped
pinch of dried chilli flakes
salt and freshly ground black pepper
wild rocket salad, to serve

1 Preheat the oven to 190°C (375°F/Gas 5). Brush 2 baking sheets with oil. With a sharp knife, score a crisscross pattern on the flesh of each butternut squash half and brush with the oil. Sit the squash on the greased baking sheets, flesh-side down, and roast for about 1 hour until the flesh begins to soften. Now scoop out most of the flesh, leaving a thin layer still attached to the skins, and reserve the hollowed squash halves.

2 Place the flesh in a bowl and mash with a fork. Add all the fruit and nut mix ingredients to the mashed squash and mix well. Divide the mixture between the squash skins.

3 Sprinkle over the cheese and return the squash halves to the oven. Bake for a further 10–15 minutes until the cheese is bubbling. Serve the squash with a lightly dressed wild rocket salad.

GREAT FOR KiDS

PIZZA MARGHERITA

SERVES 4   **PREP** 20 MINS   **COOK** 20-25 MINS
PLUS RISING

Add different toppings to this basic recipe: wilted spinach and ricotta; sliced mushrooms and Parma ham; pepperoni and chilli, sprinkled with rocket after baking.

oil, for greasing
450g (1lb) gluten-free white
  bread flour blend (see page 24),
  plus extra for dusting
1 tsp xanthan gum
2 tsp fast-action dried yeast
2 tsp caster sugar
1 tsp salt
1 egg
2 tbsp olive oil, plus extra to drizzle
300g (10oz) mozzarella cheese,
  drained and torn into pieces

a few black olives
basil leaves

For the tomato sauce
2 tbsp olive oil
1 small onion, finely chopped
2 garlic cloves, crushed
400g can cherry tomatoes
1 tbsp tomato purée
1 tsp dried oregano
pinch of sugar
salt and freshly ground black pepper

1 Lightly oil 2 baking sheets. Sift the flour, xanthan, yeast, sugar, and salt into a large bowl. Combine 300ml (10fl oz) warm water, the egg, and 2 tablespoons oil in a jug and whisk with a fork. Make a well in the centre of the dry ingredients, add the wet ingredients, and mix well to form a dough. Turn the dough out onto a floured surface and knead for 5 minutes until smooth. Return the dough to a lightly oiled bowl and cover loosely with oiled cling film. Leave in a warm place to rise until doubled in size, about 1 hour.

2 For the tomato sauce, heat the oil in a medium pan, add the onion, and sauté over a medium heat for 5 minutes. Stir in the garlic and cook for 1 minute. Add the remaining ingredients and simmer, uncovered, for 10 minutes. Set aside.

3 Preheat the oven to 230°C (450°F/Gas 8). Knock back the dough, divide into 2 balls and roll each out to a large circle. Place on the baking sheets. Divide the sauce, mozzarella, and olives between the pizza bases. Season with black pepper and drizzle over a little oil. Bake for 10 minutes or until golden. Scatter the basil over each pizza and serve.

STATISTICS PER SERVING

Energy 759kcals/3190kJ

Protein 28g

Fat 32g
Saturated fat 13g

Carbohydrate 89g
Sugar 9g

Fibre 6g

Salt 1.9g

● ● ● CALORIES

● ● ● SATURATED FAT

● ● ○ SALT

LAVOSH WITH AUBERGINE DIP

SERVES 8   **PREP** 20 MINS   **COOK** 1 HOUR 10 MINS

Iranian-style seeded crisp breads served with a sesame-scented aubergine dip make a great snack or appetiser.

150g (5½oz) gluten-free plain
  flour, plus extra for dusting
2 tsp xanthan gum
½ tsp salt
2 egg whites
15g (½oz) butter, melted
2 tbsp sesame seeds
1 tbsp poppy seeds

For the dip
2 medium aubergines
2 garlic cloves, crushed
zest and juice of 1 lemon
3 tbsp tahini paste
½ tsp salt
90ml (3fl oz) olive oil
3 tbsp finely chopped fresh coriander
4 tbsp Greek yogurt
freshly ground black pepper

1 Preheat the oven to 200°C (400°F/Gas 6). For the dip, bake the aubergines on a baking tray for 30–40 minutes or until soft and lightly charred. Cool.

2 Meanwhile, make the lavosh. Sift the flour, xanthan, and salt into a large bowl. Beat 1 egg white with 90ml (3fl oz) water, stir into the flour with the melted butter, and mix well to form a dough. Lightly knead the dough on a floured surface, divide into 6 balls, and roll out each ball until paper thin, then place on baking sheets. Repeat with all the dough.

3 Brush the remaining egg white over the lavosh, sprinkle the seeds, and bake in 2 batches for 10–15 minutes or until crisp and golden.

4 Halve the aubergines and scoop the flesh into a food processor. Add the rest of the ingredients and blend to a chunky spread. Check the seasoning, spoon into a bowl, and serve with the crisp breads.

COOK'S TIP
You can also store the lavosh, after it has cooled, in an airtight container for 2–3 days. Re-crisp in a warm oven. The dip can be stored for 2–3 days in an airtight container in the fridge.

STATISTICS PER SERVING

Energy 226kcals/994kJ

Protein 5.5g

Fat 17g
Saturated fat 3.5g

Carbohydrate 15.5g
Sugar 1.5g

Fibre 3g

Salt 0.6g

● ● ○ CALORIES

● ● ● SATURATED FAT

● ● ○ SALT

BREADSTICKS WITH PEPPER DIP

MAKES 18   **PREP** 15 MINS   **COOK** 45–50 MINS
PLUS RISING

These party nibbles come in three different flavours,
but if preferred, simply dust with polenta.

350g (12oz) gluten-free white bread
   flour blend (see page 24), plus extra
   for dusting
2 tsp fast-action dried yeast
2 tsp xanthan gum
2 tsp caster sugar
1 tsp salt
2 eggs
2 tbsp olive oil
vegetable oil, for brushing
4 tbsp poppy seeds
4 tbsp sesame seeds
6 tbsp finely grated Parmesan cheese

For the roasted pepper dip
2 large red peppers
4 garlic cloves, unpeeled
3 tbsp olive oil
1 tsp smoked paprika
½ tsp caster sugar
½ tsp ground cumin
½ tsp salt
dash of Tabasco sauce

1 Preheat the oven to 220°C (425°F/Gas 7). Sift the flour, yeast, xanthan,
sugar, and salt into a large bowl. Lightly beat 1 egg with the olive oil and
250ml (9fl oz) lukewarm water, add to the dry ingredients, and mix to form
a dough. Transfer to a lightly floured surface and knead for 5 minutes.
Return to the bowl, cover with oiled cling film, and leave to rise in a warm
place for about 1 hour until doubled in size.

2 Meanwhile, roast the peppers on a baking tray for 15–20 minutes until
lightly charred. Add the garlic and cook for a further 10 minutes. Transfer
the peppers and garlic to a plastic bag and leave to cool. Core and deseed
the peppers and peel off the skin. Pop the garlic from their skins. Combine
with the remaining ingredients in a food processor and blitz to a coarse dip.

3 Lightly oil 2 baking sheets. Roll out the dough to a fat sausage and cut
into 18 equal-sized pieces. Roll each piece into a stick 12cm (5in) long. Scatter
the seeds and Parmesan onto 3 separate plates. Beat the remaining egg.
Brush the sticks with the beaten egg and roll a third of the sticks in each
flavour. Place them a little apart on the baking sheets and bake for 15–20
minutes or until crisp and golden. Allow to cool.

STATISTICS PER SERVING

Energy 158kcals/662kJ

Protein 6g

Fat 9.5g
Saturated fat 2.5g

Carbohydrate 16g
Sugar 2.5g

Fibre 1.5g

Salt 0.4g

CHEESE STRAWS WITH TOMATO AND BASIL DIP

GUIDELINES PER SERVING

● ● ○ CALORIES

● ● ● SATURATED FAT

● ● ○ SALT

MAKES 18   **PREP** 15 MINS   **COOK** 15-20 MINS
PLUS CHILLING

Shape the cheese straw trimmings into little biscuits – they still taste great, whatever the shape.

225g (8oz) gluten-free plain flour, plus extra for dusting
100g (3½oz) butter, cubed
2 tsp mustard powder
1 tsp xanthan gum
½ tsp salt
85g (3oz) mature Cheddar cheese, grated, or blue cheese, crumbled
1 egg, beaten
milk for brushing

3 tbsp finely grated Parmesan cheese
paprika, for sprinkling

For the dip
4 medium tomatoes
2 tbsp finely chopped basil
1 tbsp olive oil
1 tbsp tomato purée
½ tsp caster sugar
salt and freshly ground black pepper

1 Place the flour, butter, mustard, xanthan, and salt in a food processor and pulse until the mixture looks like crumbs. Transfer to a bowl. Stir through the Cheddar or blue cheese, then add the egg along with 4 tablespoons cold water. Using a round-bladed knife, mix to form a ball of dough. Lightly knead on a floured surface, wrap in cling film, and chill for 30 minutes.

2 Preheat the oven to 200°C (400°F/Gas 6). Roll out the dough on a lightly floured surface to a rectangle measuring 23 x 36cm (9 x 14½in), and trim the edges. Brush with milk, then sprinkle over the Parmesan and paprika. Cut 2cm (¾in) wide strips from the dough and place them on baking trays. Bake for 15–20 minutes or until the strips are golden and puffy. Leave to cool.

3 For the dip, score the tomatoes and soak in boiling water for 30 seconds. Peel and discard the skin, then roughly chop the tomatoes on a board to make a pulp. Tip the flesh and all the juices into a small bowl. Add the remaining ingredients, stir well, and season to taste. Serve at room temperature with the cheese straws.

STATISTICS PER SERVING

Energy	133kcals/554kJ
Protein	4g
Fat	8.5g
Saturated fat	5g
Carbohydrate	10g
Sugar	1g
Fibre	0.8g
Salt	0.4g

● ● ○ CALORIES

● ● ● SATURATED FAT

● ● ○ SALT

GREAT FOR KIDS

SPICY PEPPER EMPANADAS

SERVES 5   **PREP** 30 MINS   **COOK** 30 MINS   **FREEZE** 1 MONTH
UNCOOKED

A variety of savoury or sweet fillings – pumpkin and cheese to mixed berries – work well in this South American snack.

1 tbsp olive oil
1 large onion, sliced
salt and freshly ground black pepper
1 red pepper, deseeded and chopped
2 garlic cloves, finely chopped
3 red or green jalapeños, chopped
2 tbsp dry sherry
300g can chickpeas, drained
2 tbsp finely chopped fresh coriander

2 tbsp finely chopped flat-leaf parsley
100g (3½oz) butter
juice of 1 lemon
225g (8oz) gluten-free plain flour, plus
   extra for dusting
1 tsp paprika
sunflower oil, for frying

SPECIAL EQUIPMENT food processor

1 For the filling, heat the oil in a medium pan, add the onion, and season. Cook on a low heat for 2–3 minutes until soft. Add the red pepper, garlic, and jalapeños, and cook for 10 minutes or until the pepper starts to soften Add the sherry to the pan, raise the heat, and cook for 2 minutes. Tip in the chickpeas, coriander, and parsley, and stir. Season to taste. Transfer to a food processor and pulse to break it up, but not mince it.

2 To make the pastry, melt the butter in a pan, add the lemon juice and 100ml (3½fl oz) water. Combine the flour, 1 teaspoon salt, and paprika in a mixing bowl. Add the melted butter liquid and mix to a thick paste. Knead gently for 2 minutes. Leave to rest for 2–3 minutes at room temperature.

3 To form the empanadas, roll the pastry out on a floured surface to about 3mm (⅛in) thick, adding more flour if needed. Cut out 10 rounds, 10cm (4in) in diameter. Spoon a generous amount of filling onto one half of each round, wet around the edges with water, fold over, and seal with a pinch.

4 Pour sunflower oil into a small, deep-sided frying pan, to a depth of 1cm (½in), and heat to medium. Add 3 empanadas at a time and cook for 2–3 minutes on each side until golden. Transfer to a plate lined with kitchen paper. Serve hot or warm.

STATISTICS PER SERVING

Energy 424kcals/1774kJ

Protein 8g

Fat 24g
Saturated fat 12g

Carbohydrate 42g
Sugar 4g

Fibre 3g

Salt 1.2g

● ● ○ CALORIES

● ○ ○ SATURATED FAT

● ● ○ SALT

VEGETABLE SPRING ROLLS

MAKES 10 **PREP** 30 MINS **COOK** 15–20 MINS

You can fry these ahead and crisp them up in a hot oven just before serving. Look for rice pancakes in Asian stores.

15g (½oz) dried shiitake mushrooms, soaked in boiling water for 20 mins
1 small carrot, cut into matchsticks
3 spring onions, cut into matchsticks
85g (3oz) white cabbage, shredded
2 garlic cloves, crushed
2cm (¾in) piece of fresh root ginger, peeled and grated
2 tbsp tamari (gluten-free soy sauce)
1 tbsp Chinese cooking wine
½ tsp Chinese five-spice powder
1 tbsp vegetable oil

60g (2oz) beansprouts
20 rice pancakes
vegetable oil, for deep-frying

For the chilli dipping sauce
60g (2oz) caster sugar
90ml (3fl oz) rice wine vinegar
2 garlic cloves, chopped
2 red chillies, finely chopped

SPECIAL EQUIPMENT deep-fat fryer, or large pan plus cooking thermometer

1 Drain and finely chop the mushrooms and mix together with the next 5 ingredients. In a small jug, mix the tamari, wine, and five-spice powder. Heat the oil in a frying pan or wok, add the vegetable mix, mushrooms, and beansprouts, and stir-fry for 1 minute. Add the tamari mix and simmer for 30 seconds. Remove from the heat and leave to cool.

2 For the sauce, place the ingredients in a medium pan with 4 tablespoons water, boil, then simmer for 5 minutes or until slightly thickened. Cool.

3 Dip a pancake in a bowl of warm water for 10–15 seconds or until soft. Lay it on a damp tea towel and blot until slightly sticky. Place a heaped dessertspoonful of filling in the centre. Fold the bottom of the pancake up over the filling, fold in the sides, rolling up the pancake tightly. Soak a second pancake, wrap it around the first layer, and set aside. Repeat until the filling is used up. Heat the oil in a deep-fat fryer or large pan until it reaches 180°C (350°F). Do not leave the fryer or pan unattended, switch off when not using, and keep a fire blanket nearby in case of fire. Cook the spring rolls in the hot oil, 2 at a time, for 3–4 minutes or until golden. Remove with a slotted spoon and drain on kitchen paper. Keep warm while you fry the remainder. Serve the rolls hot with the chilli dipping sauce.

STATISTICS PER ROLL

Energy 105kcals/440kJ

Protein 1.1g

Fat 6g
Saturated fat 0.7g

Carbohydrate 12g
Sugar 8g

Fibre 1g

Salt 0.7g

VEGETABLE CRISPS

SERVES 4   **PREP** 20 MINS   **COOK** 30 MINS

Deliciously sweet and healthier than regular crisps, these make an ideal snack for children; omit the salt if you prefer.

2 parsnips
1 sweet potato
2 beetroots

sunflower oil, for deep-frying,
  enough to fill half the pan
sea salt (optional)

1 Peel and trim the vegetables, then cut them into wafer-thin slices using a vegetable peeler or a mandolin, if you have one.

2 Heat the oil in a heavy, deep-sided pan over a high heat until really hot. Don't leave the pan unattended, take off the heat when not using, and keep a fire blanket nearby in case of fire. Add the vegetable slices a few at a time. Fry each batch for 2–3 minutes or until crisp and golden, then remove with a slotted spoon and spread out over kitchen paper on a baking sheet. Repeat until all are cooked.

3 Sprinkle with sea salt (if using) and then sit them piled high in bowls to serve with drinks, or serve alongside meat such as game.

VARIATIONS
Sprinkle with either paprika, black pepper, or dried chilli flakes for extra flavour.

Yellow beetroot »
If you are wary of the staining juices from red beetroot, look out for Burpee's Golden, a bright yellow beet that does not bleed when cut.

GREAT FOR KIDS

NUTRIENT BOOST
Beetroots produce nitric oxide gas in the blood, which lowers blood pressure.

STATISTICS PER SERVING

Energy 258kcals/1076kJ

Protein 3g

Fat 17.5g
Saturated fat 2g

Carbohydrate 22g
Sugar 10g

Fibre 7.5g

Salt 0.15g

CORN AND FETA FRITTERS

SERVES 4   **PREP** 15 MINS   **COOK** 15 MINS   **FREEZE** 1 MONTH
PLUS RESTING

A very easy, light supper dish that uses only a few
ingredients from the fridge and storecupboard.

125g (4½oz) gluten-free plain flour
2 tsp gluten-free baking powder
1 egg
100ml (3½fl oz) milk
195g can sweetcorn, drained, or the
  kernels from 2 fresh cobs (see below)

freshly ground black pepper
75g (2½oz) feta cheese, crumbled
2-3 tbsp sunflower oil, for frying
fried or grilled bacon, to serve
  (optional)

1 Sift the flour and baking powder into a bowl and make a well. Add the
egg and milk, and start to incorporate the flour, whisking until smooth. Add
the sweetcorn, some pepper, and mix. Rest in the fridge for 15 minutes.

2 When ready to cook, stir in the feta, then heat a little oil in a non-stick
frying pan over a medium heat. Spoon in 2 tablespoons of the mixture and
flatten together to form each fritter, leaving plenty of space between them;
you will have to cook them in batches.

3 Fry for 1–2 minutes or until the underside is pale golden, then turn and
cook the other side for a further 1–2 minutes. Remove and drain on kitchen
paper. Serve alone or with bacon, as a main meal or breakfast.

VARIATIONS
Once you've mastered the batter mix, try varying it with grated Cheddar cheese
and spring onion, peas and chopped mint, or blue cheese and chopped red onion.

Corn on the cob »
To prepare fresh sweetcorn, pull off
the husk and silk, hold upright, and slice
straight down the sides to cut off the
kernels. Steam or boil for 2-3 minutes.

GREAT FOR KiDS

NUTRIENT BOOST
The phytochemicals in
canned sweetcorn are
more easily absorbed
than in fresh.

STATISTICS PER SERVING

Energy 294kcals/1230kJ

Protein 8g

Fat 13g
Saturated fat 4.5g

Carbohydrate 36g
Sugar 5.5g

Fibre 0.8g

Salt 1.9g

BROWN BREAD

MAKES 12 SLICES **PREP** 20 MINS **COOK** 35–40 MINS **FREEZE** 3 MONTHS
PLUS RISING

A spongy and moist gluten-free loaf that rises well and has a good colour and flavour. This dough can also be used to make a tasty, seeded loaf (see Variation).

oil, for greasing
450g (1lb) gluten-free brown bread flour blend (see page 24), plus extra for dusting
2 tsp fast-action dried yeast
½ tsp salt
2 tbsp black treacle

1 egg
2 tbsp vegetable oil
1 tsp vinegar
beaten egg, for brushing

SPECIAL EQUIPMENT 450g (1lb) loaf tin

1 Lightly oil the tin. Sift the flour into a large bowl and add the yeast and salt. Measure 300ml (10fl oz) lukewarm water into a jug and add the treacle, egg, vegetable oil, and vinegar. Whisk together with a fork.

2 Make a well in the centre of the dry ingredients, add the wet ingredients, and mix well to form a dough. Turn onto a lightly floured surface and knead for about 5 minutes until smooth.

3 Shape the dough into a rectangle the same size as the tin and place in the prepared tin. Cover loosely with oiled cling film and leave in a warm place to rise for 1 hour or until doubled in size.

4 Preheat the oven to 200°C (400°F/Gas 6). Brush the top of the loaf with the beaten egg and bake in the oven for 35–40 minutes or until it is risen and golden brown. Remove from the oven and allow to cool for 5 minutes in the tin, then turn out and cool on a wire rack.

STATISTICS PER SLICE

Energy 222kcals/941kJ

Protein 8g

Fat 5g

Saturated fat 2g

Carbohydrate 36g

Sugar 3.5g

Fibre 7g

Salt 0.3g

VARIATION

Seeded loaf Simply sprinkle a mix of seeds (poppy, pumpkin, and sunflower are all good) into the oiled tin before adding the dough. Once risen, finish with a final flourish of more seeds after brushing with egg.

○○○ CALORIES

○○○ SATURATED FAT

○○○ SALT

CARAWAY SEED BREAD

MAKES 12 SLICES   **PREP** 20 MINS   **COOK** 40-50 MINS   **FREEZE** 1 MONTH
PLUS RISING

This crunchy, crusty loaf, peppered with caraway seeds, is particularly good served with cured meats and cheese.

oil, for greasing
450g (1lb) gluten-free white
  bread flour blend (see page 24)
2 tsp fast-action dried yeast
2 tsp salt
2 tbsp light soft brown sugar
2 tsp caraway seeds

300ml (10fl oz) milk
2 eggs
2 tbsp vegetable oil
1 tsp balsamic vinegar
2 tsp caster sugar

SPECIAL EQUIPMENT 900g (2lb) loaf tin

1 Lightly oil the loaf tin. Sift the flour, yeast, and 1 teaspoon salt into a large bowl. Stir in the sugar and 1 teaspoon of the caraway seeds. Heat the milk until lukewarm (see Cook's tip). Add one of the eggs, the oil, and vinegar to the milk, and whisk with a fork. Make a well in the centre of the dry ingredients, add the wet ingredients, and mix well to form a dough. Knead on a lightly floured surface for 5 minutes, until smooth.

2 Shape the dough into a fat roll and transfer to the tin. Use a sharp knife to make diagonal slashes across the dough. Cover loosely with oiled cling film and leave in a warm place to rise for 1 hour or until doubled in size.

3 Preheat the oven to 220°C (425°F/Gas 7). To glaze, beat together the remaining egg, salt, and caster sugar, generously brush it over the loaf, and sprinkle the remaining caraway seeds. Bake for 35–40 minutes or until the loaf is risen and golden brown. Remove from the tin and bake for a further 5–10 minutes to crisp the crust. Remove from the oven and cool on a wire rack.

STATISTICS PER SLICE

Energy 190kcals/802kJ

Protein 6g

Fat 4.5g
Saturated fat 1g

Carbohydrate 31.5g
Sugar 5g

Fibre 1.6g

Salt 0.7g

COOK'S TIP
The ideal temperature for yeast to work is 35°C (95°F). Temperatures above 60°C (140°F) will kill the yeast, so it's important the milk is heated until warm but not hot to the touch.

CALORIES

SATURATED FAT

SALT

PUMPKIN BREAD WREATH

SERVES 12 **PREP** 25 MINS **COOK** 1 HOUR 5 MINS–1¼ HOURS
PLUS RISING

Gently spiced, this lovely moist bread makes an impressive centrepiece for a party, especially around Hallowe'en.

vegetable oil, for greasing
500g (1lb 2oz) pumpkin or butternut squash, peeled, deseeded, and cut into 5cm (2in) cubes, or 400g (14oz) canned pumpkin purée
2 tbsp olive oil
salt and freshly ground black pepper
675g (1½lb) gluten-free white bread flour blend (see page 24) plus extra for dusting
2 tsp xanthan gum

1 tbsp fast-action dried yeast
2½ tsp salt
1 tsp ground cinnamon
1 tsp ground ginger
½ tsp ground cloves
60g (2oz) light soft brown sugar
30g (1oz) butter
200ml (7fl oz) milk
2 large eggs
1 tsp caster sugar
2 tbsp pumpkin seeds

1 Oil a large baking sheet. Place the butternut cubes in a roasting tin and drizzle over the olive oil, 3 tablespoons water, and seasoning. Cover with foil and roast for 30–35 minutes or until tender. Transfer to a food processor and whizz until smooth. Spread in the roasting tin and leave until cold.

2 Sift the flour, xanthan, yeast, 1½ teaspoons salt, and the spices into a large bowl and stir in the brown sugar. Melt the butter in a pan, add the milk and heat to lukewarm, then add 1 egg and beat with a fork. Pour the wet mixture over the dry ingredients, add the squash, and mix to form a dough. Knead the dough on a lightly floured surface for 5 minutes until smooth. Roll it into 12 even-sized balls. Place 9 of these in a circle on a large, oiled baking sheet and 3 in the centre to make a wreath. Cover with oiled cling film and leave in a warm place for 1 hour or until doubled in size.

3 Preheat the oven to 200°C (400°F/Gas 6). Beat the remaining egg, caster sugar, and 1 teaspoon salt, and brush over the rolls. Scatter over the pumpkin seeds and bake for 35–40 minutes until golden brown. Cool for 30 minutes. Serve the bread warm on a large board, so guests can break off the rolls.

STATISTICS PER SERVING

Energy 304kcals/1283kJ

Protein 8g

Fat 8g

Saturated fat 2.5g

Carbohydrate 50g

Sugar 9g

Fibre 3.5g

Salt 0.9g

⬤⬤◯ CALORIES

⬤◯◯ SATURATED FAT

⬤◯◯ SALT

APRICOT AND CARDAMOM TEABREAD

SERVES 12   **PREP** 15 MINS   **COOK** 1¼–1½ HOURS   **FREEZE** 2 MONTHS

Earl Grey tea adds a lovely citrus note to this wonderfully moist teabread, but any other tea will work too.

1 tea bag, such as Earl Grey
225g (8oz) ready-to-eat dried apricots, finely chopped
6 cardamom pods, split
175g (6oz) light muscovado sugar
oil, for greasing
225g (8oz) gluten-free plain flour
1 tsp gluten-free baking powder
1 tsp xanthan gum
1 tsp ground cinnamon

pinch of salt
75g (2½oz) cold unslated butter, cubed
2 eggs, beaten
15g (½oz) flaked almonds
2 tbsp demerara sugar
butter, to serve

SPECIAL EQUIPMENT
900g (2lb) loaf tin

1 Pour 300ml (10fl oz) boiling water over the tea bag and leave to infuse for 5 minutes. Place the apricots in a small pan. Remove the tea bag and add the hot tea, cardamom, and sugar to the pan. Bring to the boil, then simmer, uncovered, for 10 minutes. Leave until cold; the apricot mixture will cool quickly if tipped into a shallow tray. Remove the cardamom pods.

2 Preheat the oven to 180°C (350°F/Gas 4). Lightly oil the tin and line the base with baking parchment. Sift the flour, baking powder, xanthan, cinnamon, and salt into a large bowl. Rub the butter into the flour mixture. Stir the cold apricots and their cooking liquid into the flour, add the eggs, and beat together. Pour into the tin and scatter over the almonds and demerara sugar. Bake in the centre of the oven for 1 hour 20–25 minutes or until well risen and firm to the touch.

3 Cool in the tin for 10 minutes before transferring to a wire rack to cool completely. The tea bread is even better the day after baking and will keep in an airtight container for up to 1 week.

STATISTICS PER SLICE

Energy   225kcals/948kJ

Protein   4g

Fat   7g

Saturated fat   3.5g

Carbohydrate   36g

Sugar   23g

Fibre   2.4g

Salt   0.3g

● ● ● CALORIES

● ● ● SATURATED FAT

● ● ○ SALT

APRICOT FRANGIPANE TART

SERVES 10   **PREP** 20 MINS   **COOK** 25-35 MINS

An impressive dessert of crisp buttery pastry filled with a sweet almond paste and topped with apricots.

250g (9oz) gluten-free shortcrust pastry (see pages 20-21)
gluten-free plain flour, for dusting

For the filling
200g (7oz) butter
200g (7oz) caster sugar
1 tsp vanilla extract

5 egg yolks
200g (7oz) ground almonds
4-5 ripe apricots, halved and stoned
crème fraîche, to serve

SPECIAL EQUIPMENT 25cm (10in) round, loose-bottomed tart tin

1 Preheat the oven to 200°C (400°F/Gas 6). Roll the pastry out on a lightly floured surface to a 35cm (14in) circle, about 3mm (⅛in) thick. Place it into the base of the tin, with the edges overlapping, patching up any tears in the pastry. Ease it into the corners and sides of the tin, and trim the edges. Prick the base with a fork, line with baking parchment, and fill with baking beans. Bake for 15 minutes or until the edges begin to turn golden. Remove from the oven, take out the beans and paper, and return to the oven for 5 more minutes. Set aside. Reduce the oven temperature to 180°C (350°F/Gas 4).

2 To make the filling, beat the butter in a large bowl with an electric whisk for 2 minutes. Add the sugar and beat until pale and creamy. Add the vanilla extract and mix. Now add the egg yolks, one at a time, and beat gently until they are all incorporated. Gently stir through the ground almonds.

3 Pour the filling into the pastry case and arrange the apricots, cut side down, in the mixture, pressing them in slightly so they fit snugly. Bake for 25–35 minutes or until the mixture is cooked and golden. Leave to cool and serve at room temperature with crème fraîche.

VARIATIONS
Try other seasonal fruits like peaches, blackberries, or stoned cherries. For a sweeter tart, spread the pastry base with strawberry or raspberry jam before filling.

STATISTICS PER SLICE

Energy 499kcals/2079kJ

Protein 7.5g

Fat 37.4g

Saturated fat 14g

Carbohydrate 33g

Sugar 25g

Fibre 1g

Salt 0.6g

GREAT FOR KiDS

BLACKBERRY AND APPLE PIE

SERVES 6   **PREP** 15 MINS   **COOK** 40–50 MINS   **FREEZE** 3 MONTHS
PLUS CHILLING

A classic pie using late summer fruits. Omit the spices and serve with gluten-free ice cream to make this perfect for kids.

450g (1lb) gluten-free shortcrust
  pastry (see pages 20-21)
gluten-free plain flour, for dusting
1 egg, lightly beaten
1 tbsp caster sugar

For the filling
3 cooking apples, peeled, cored,
  and sliced
1 star anise

1 vanilla pod, split lengthways
pinch of freshly grated nutmeg
100g (3½oz) demerara sugar
250g (9oz) blackberries
zest of ½ lemon or ½ orange

SPECIAL EQUIPMENT
18cm (7in) round pie dish

1 Set aside one-third of the pastry for the lid. On a lightly floured surface, roll out the remaining pastry into a circle large enough to line the pie dish and overlap the sides. Chill in the fridge while you prepare the filling.

2 Place the apple slices in a pan with 6 tablespoons cold water, add the star anise, vanilla pod, nutmeg, and half the sugar, and cook over a very gentle heat for 10–15 minutes until the apples begin to soften. Remove from the heat and set aside for 20 minutes to allow the flavours to infuse.

3 Sprinkle the pastry base with the remaining sugar. Remove the vanilla pod, star anise, and any excess liquid from the apples. Arrange the apple slices over the pastry, then add the blackberries and lemon or orange zest.

4 Wet the edges of the pastry with a little water. Roll out the pastry for the lid and drape, pressing the edges to seal. Trim the edges and slash the top a couple of times. Brush with half the egg and chill for 20 minutes.

5 Preheat the oven to 200°C (400°F/Gas 6). Brush the pie with the remaining egg and sprinkle with caster sugar. Bake for 40–50 minutes until golden. If it starts to brown too much, cover the top with a little foil, as you need the underside of the pastry to cook. Leave to cool slightly and serve warm.

STATISTICS PER SLICE

Energy 323kcals/1362kJ

Protein 4.5g

Fat 13g

Saturated fat 4g

Carbohydrate 47g

Sugar 30g

Fibre 5g

Salt 0.5g

RASPBERRY AND WHITE CHOCOLATE TRIFLE

SERVES 6 **PREP** 20 MINS
PLUS COOLING

Tart raspberries contrast well with sweet white chocolate, and a trickle of cassis liqueur transforms this dessert into an indulgent, special occasion trifle.

200g (7oz) white chocolate, broken into even-sized pieces, plus extra for grating to decorate
175g (6oz) gluten-free sponge or amaretti biscuits crumbled
juice of 1–2 oranges

2 tbsp cassis (optional)
300ml (10fl oz) double cream, lightly whipped, or mascarpone cheese
300g (10oz) raspberries
50g (1¾oz) flaked almonds, lightly toasted

1 Put the chocolate in a heatproof bowl over a pan of barely simmering water and stir occasionally until melted. Remove the bowl from the pan and leave to cool slightly.

2 Place the crumbled sponge or biscuits in the base of a glass serving dish. Pour over just enough orange juice to wet the sponge, then add half the cassis (if using). Set aside for the sponge or biscuits to absorb the juice.

3 Mix the melted chocolate with half the whipped cream or mascarpone and stir well to combine. Mix the remaining cassis with the raspberries. Reserve some raspberries for decoration. Spoon half the cream mixture into the dish and top with half the raspberry mixture. Repeat the layers to use the remaining cream and raspberry mixture. Top with the leftover cream and dot with the reserved raspberries, then sprinkle over the almonds and grated white chocolate. Chill before serving.

COOK'S TIP
A variety of bases can be used for the trifle – try gluten-free brownies, biscuits, or fruit cake for a heavier version – and try stewed fruits for a winter pudding.

STATISTICS PER SERVING

Energy 644kcals/2676kJ

Protein 8g

Fat 50g

Saturated fat 25g

Carbohydrate 39g

Sugar 33g

Fibre 2g

Salt 0.4g

CALORIES

SATURATED FAT

SALT

CHOCOLATE CHEESECAKE

SERVES 8   **PREP** 20 MINS   **COOK** 35–40 MINS
PLUS COOLING

A gooey mixture of dark chocolate and mascarpone baked on a crumbly base of almond or ginger biscuits.

85g (3oz) butter, plus
  extra for greasing
175g (6oz) gluten-free ginger
  or amaretti biscuits crushed
150g (5½oz) dark chocolate
  (70% cocoa solids), broken
  into even-sized pieces
2 eggs, separated
pinch of salt

400g (14oz) mascarpone cheese
zest and juice of 1 orange
115g (4oz) caster sugar
2 tbsp cornflour
double cream, to serve

SPECIAL EQUIPMENT
20cm (8in) round springform cake tin

1 Preheat the oven to 180°C (350°F/Gas 4). Grease the tin and line with baking parchment. Gently melt the butter in a pan, remove from the heat, and stir in the crushed biscuits. Press the buttery biscuit mixture into the base and edges of the tin, using the back of a wooden spoon to smooth it out. Leave to cool then chill in the fridge.

2 Meanwhile, put the chocolate in a heatproof bowl set over a pan of barely simmering water and stir occasionally until melted. Remove the bowl from the pan and leave the chocolate to cool slightly.

3 Place the egg whites and salt in a bowl and whisk until stiff. Set aside.

4 Place the mascarpone, melted chocolate, orange zest and juice, caster sugar, and egg yolks in a large bowl and beat gently with an electric whisk to combine. Fold in the cornflour and then the egg whites.

5 Pour the mixture over the biscuit base and spread it until even and smooth. Bake for 35–40 minutes or until firm to the touch. Switch off the heat and leave the cheesecake to cool inside the oven; this helps prevent cracking. Once cool, remove from the oven and set aside until completely cold, then release the sides and ease from the tin. Serve with a drizzle of double cream.

STATISTICS PER SLICE

Energy 598kcals/2501kJ

Protein 7g

Fat 43g

Saturated fat 23.5g

Carbohydrate 41g

Sugar 41g

Fibre 0.6g

Salt 0.4g

● ● ● CALORIES

● ● ● SATURATED FAT

● ○ ○ SALT

CHOCOLATE CAKE

SERVES 12   **PREP** 25–30 MINS   **COOK** 25–30 MINS   **FREEZE** 3 MONTHS

This light-as-a-feather sponge, smothered in a wickedly delicious chocolate fudge icing, makes for the perfect treat.

butter, for greasing
200g (7oz) dark chocolate, broken
  into pieces
310g (11oz) unsalted butter, softened
225g (8oz) light muscovado sugar
3 eggs, separated
100g (3½oz) gluten-free
  self-raising flour
½ tsp gluten-free bicarbonate of soda

60g (2oz) cocoa powder
60g (2oz) ground almonds
4 tbsp milk
120ml (4fl oz) double cream
200g (7oz) icing sugar, sifted

SPECIAL EQUIPMENT
2 x 20cm (8in) round cake tins

1 Preheat the oven to 180°C (350°F/Gas 4). Grease the tins and line with baking parchment. Melt 60g (2oz) of the chocolate in a heatproof bowl over a pan of simmering water. Cool slightly.

2 In a large bowl, cream together 225g (8oz) of the butter and muscovado sugar with an electric whisk until light and fluffy. Add the egg yolks and cooled chocolate and whisk again. Sift in the flour, soda, and cocoa. Add the almonds and milk and gently fold in until well mixed. Whisk the egg whites in a clean bowl to form stiff peaks. Stir a large spoonful into the chocolate mix, then gently fold in the remainder.

3 Divide the mixture between the 2 tins and bake in the centre of the oven for 25–30 minutes or until the sponges bounce back when lightly touched in the centre. Place the tins on a wire rack and cover with a damp tea towel, which will keep them beautifully moist. Leave until cold.

4 For the icing, combine the remaining chocolate and the cream in a large bowl and place over a pan of gently simmering water. Stir occasionally until the chocolate has melted and the mixture is smooth. Remove and cool. In a separate bowl, whisk the remaining butter with the icing sugar until fluffy, add the melted chocolate mixture, and whisk until smooth. Turn out the sponges. Spread a third of the icing over one sponge and top with the second. Spread the remaining icing over the top and sides of the cake.

STATISTICS PER SLICE

Energy 565kcals/2359kJ

Protein 6g

Fat 37g
Saturated fat 21g

Carbohydrate 52g
Sugar 46g

Fibre 2g

Salt 0.8g

● ● ● CALORIES

● ● ● SATURATED FAT

● ● ○ SALT

CARAMELIZED ORANGE PUDDING

SERVES 10   **PREP** 20 MINS   **COOK** 30–40 MINS

Be patient when baking this tangy, orange-topped sponge. Don't open the oven for a peep too early or the pudding won't rise and it may even sink.

275g (9½oz) unsalted butter, plus extra for greasing
3-4 oranges, peeled, pith and pips removed, and thickly sliced
3-4 tbsp demerara sugar
115g (4oz) gluten-free self-raising flour
1 tsp gluten-free baking powder

1 tsp xanthan gum
175g (6oz) golden caster sugar
3 eggs
3 tbsp milk
double cream, crème fraîche, or gluten-free custard to serve

1 Preheat the oven to 180°C (350°F/Gas 4). Grease an 18 x 30cm (7 x 12in) ovenproof dish with a little butter. Melt 100g (3½oz) butter in a large, non-stick frying pan over a medium heat. Add the orange slices and demerara sugar, and cook for 5–6 minutes until the oranges are golden and caramelized. Don't let the sugar burn. Put the oranges and sauce into the ovenproof dish.

2 Sift the flour, baking powder, and xanthan into a large bowl and set aside. Place the remaining butter and caster sugar into a bowl and beat with an electric whisk until light and fluffy. Do this for at least 8 minutes so it is really light. Add the eggs, one at a time, with a spoonful of the flour mixture. Beat until well incorporated, then fold in the remaining flour mix, and stir in the milk.

3 Spoon the mixture over the oranges and bake for 30–40 minutes, or until risen and golden and an inserted skewer comes out clean. Spoon into shallow bowls with the orange slices on top. Serve with double cream, crème fraîche, or gluten-free custard.

COOK'S TIP
This is a great pudding for children, best when served with gluten-free custard.

STATISTICS PER SERVING

Energy 643kcals/2646kJ

Protein 7g

Fat 42g

Saturated fat 25g

Carbohydrate 57g

Sugar 44g

Fibre 3g

Salt 0.9g

ABOUT THE AUTHORS

Heather Whinney is an experienced food writer and home economist. She has worked as a food editor and freelance food writer for several magazines including *BBC Good Food, Family Circle, Good Housekeeping, Prima,* and *Woman and Home.* She is the author of DK's *Cook Express* and co-author of *The Diabetes Cooking Book.* Her food philosophy has always been to write simple recipes for the everyday cook.

Jane Lawrie has been baking ever since she could stand on a chair. As an experienced food stylist and cookery writer, she has worked for numerous food and women's magazines, including *BBC Good Food, Bella, Best,* and *Good Housekeeping.* Jane also works as a consultant for the British Egg Information Service. She has worked on several DK books including *The Preserving Book* and *The Allotment Cookbook Through the Year,* as well as several *Mary Berry* and *Masterchef* cookery books.

Fiona Hunter is a food writer and nutritionist of over 25 years' experience. With a degree in Nutrition and a postgraduate diploma in Dietetics, she began her career as a dietitian in the NHS before going on to write for magazines including *BBC Good Food, Good Housekeeping,* and *Health and Fitness,* as well as making many appearances on television and radio. She is the co-author of several books, including DK's *The Diabetes Cooking Book.*

ACKNOWLEDGEMENTS

Dorling Kindersley would like to thank:

Recipe editors Jane Bamforth, Holly Kyte **Recipe testers** Rebecca Blackstone, Anna Burges-Lumsden, Amy Carter, Jan Fullwood, Laura Fyfe, Katy Greenwood, Anne Harnan, Catherine Rose, Rachel Wood **Proofreader** Sue Morony **Indexer** Sue Bosanko **Photography art direction and props styling** Luis Peral-Aranda, Katherine Raj **Food stylists** Marie-Ange Lapierre, Emily Jonzen Charis Bhagianathan and David Fentiman for editorial assistance. Mahua Mandal for design. 2012 Edition: **Senior editor** Alastair Laing **Project art editor** Katherine Raj **Managing editor** Dawn Henderson **Managing art editor** Christine Keilty **Art director** Peter Luff **DK INDIA Senior editor** Chitra Subramanyam **Editors** Divya Chandhok, Ligi John **Art editors** Prashant Kumar, Anamica Roy **Managing editor** Glenda Fernandes **Managing art editor** Navidita Thapa assistance. Danaya Bunnag for hand modelling.